# SOMEWHERE IN THE MIDDLE

# SOMEWHERE
# IN THE MIDDLE

*A journey to the Philippines in search of
roots, belonging, and identity*

DEBORAH FRANCISCO DOUGLAS

Published by Peaceful Mountain Press
www.peacefulmountainpress.com

Printed in the United States of America

First Printing, 2019

*Cover art by Ivy Pangilinan*

*Editing by Christine Schmitt, True-Blue Editing*

*This memoir is a work of creative nonfiction. The story was created from memories, journal entries, and old blog posts. All of the events that happened in this book are true, however, some dates, conversations, or chronology may not be an exact replica of actual events. Most names in this book have been changed (unless prior permission was received) in order to protect the privacy of those involved.*

ISBN 978-1-7335756-0-7

Library of Congress Control Number: 2019930213

*To my family.*

*And to all those in the Philippines who became like family.*

# Contents

# Commonly Used Terms

## Language and Cultural Terms

**Adobo** – Popular dish in the Philippines consisting of meat cooked in soy sauce and vinegar

**Ate** – Older sister (also used as term of respect for an older female)

**Bahala na** – A Filipino expression that means "it's up to God" or "it is what it is"

**Kamote** – Sweet potatoes

**CR** – Stands for Comfort Room, the Filipino term for a bathroom

**Filam** – A person who is both Filipino and American

**Filipino** – A person who is native to or who has identified a strong connection with the Philippines

**Halo-halo** – A Filipino dessert that translates to "mix-mix"

**Hay naku!** – An expression that signifies excitement, exasperation, or a sigh of frustration

**Ilocano** – Regional language spoken in many northern areas of the Philippines

**Ilonggo** – Regional dialect spoken in Iloilo City and surrounding areas

**Jeepney** – Converted metal jeep that serves as the main method of local transportation

**Kain na** – A casual way of saying "let's eat" in Tagalog

**Kasama** – Friend or companion

**Kuya** – Older brother (also used as term of respect for an older male)

**Lola** – Grandma

**Lolo** – Grandpa

**Lumpia** – Filipino style egg roll

**Mestizo/Mestiza** – A term used in the Philippines to describe someone who is half Filipino, half foreigner

**Pandesal** – Filipino sweet rolls

**Pasalubong** – Souvenir gift from another place given to a family member or friend

**Peso, or Philippine Peso (PHP)** – Currency used in the Philippines (current exchange rate as of 2019 is roughly 52 PHP = $1 USD)

**Salamat** – The Tagalog word for "thank you"

**Sari-sari** – Small convenience store found on almost every street in the Philippines

**Tagalog** – The official language of the Philippines
**Trike** – Motorized bike with a sidecar for carrying passengers, a common method of transportation for short distances
**Visayan** – Regional language spoken in the Visayan Islands

## Geographic Locations

**Baguio City** – A city located six hours north of Manila and the location of Deborah's volunteer assignment
**Benguet** – A province in the Cordillera Region where Baguio City is located
**Cordillera region** – The mountainous region of the Philippines consisting of six provinces
**Iloilo City** – The hometown of Deborah's father, located on the island of Panay in the Visayas
**Luzon** – The northern geographical area of the Philippines, largely considered to be the mainland; consists of the largest and most highly populated island of Luzon
**Manila** – The capital of the Philippines, located in Luzon
**Olongapo City** – A city located in Luzon and the site for Deborah's three-month orientation and training with the Peace Corps
**Philippines** – A small country located in Southeast Asia made up of over seven thousand islands and divided into three main geographical areas
**Province** – A political division that marks each local administrative area of governance
**Visayas (or Visayan Islands)** – The central geographical area of the Philippines consisting of several islands surrounding the Visayan Sea

*Ang hindi marunong lumingon sa pinanggalingan ay hindi makakarating sa paroroonan.*
He who does not know to look where he came from will never get to his destination.
~ Filipino saying

# 1

## 6,695 MILES FROM HOME

*October, 2013*

I sat hunched over, my chest exhausted and weak. Each breath sent pains to my chest, like I was trying to gulp for air through a slightly plugged coffee straw. I was unable to sleep. I couldn't breathe despite taking both types of my asthma medication. The state of my asthma—generally mild and under control—had become an increasing concern in the last few weeks. It didn't help that every time I went for a run in my neighborhood I would come back wheezing and blowing black snot into my Kleenex. I kept telling myself that I'd feel better soon. That's what had always happened in the past when my asthma acted up—but this time I didn't feel better.

"Get on a bus to Manila," my doctor advised over the phone after an extensive conversation about my symptoms. "Once you arrive, we can examine and treat you here."

*Manila? Now?*

Manila, the capital of the Philippines, was a six-hour bus ride down the mountains and across the lowlands from where I lived in Baguio City.

I looked at my clock—1:34 a.m.

Unsure of what to do, I started stuffing clothes into my blue-striped bag. It sat limp on my lap, just the way I felt. *Will I survive the six hours until I reach Manila?* Every few minutes I had to sit down on my bed to grip the mattress and force myself to breathe. *What am I doing taking a bus to Manila at almost two o'clock in the morning?* Then again, what was my alternative? Checking myself into a foreign hospital in Baguio City with no idea of how they would treat my medical issue scared me more than getting on a bus to a place six hours away. At least if I went to Manila, I could be treated by my American doctor. *Bus it is.*

Half an hour later I bought a ticket and boarded the air-conditioned, red Victory Liner bus. I took a seat and set my bag at my feet. I gripped the gray velvet fabric of the seat and leaned forward to make it easier to breathe. Outside my window I watched the lights of Baguio City disappear slowly into patches of fog as we descended the mountain.

It wasn't long before I started to feel lightheaded. *I need to go back to Baguio!* The further away we drove from those disappearing lights the more my mind yelled. *This is a mistake! I'm not going to make it six hours. I need to go back, now!* The bus rocked slowly back and forth as it rounded several curves on its one-way route to Manila. Slightly dizzy, I reached inside my bag for a pen and a scrap of paper.

"If I pass out, please call these numbers," I scribbled. I added my name and the phone number of my doctor and an emergency contact. I tucked the paper in the front pocket of my backpack so it could be found easily, and then I prayed silently that the trip would go smoothly. The bus rounded several more winding mountain curves, and I closed my eyes. *I need to go back.*

The red bus finally rolled into the first rest stop an hour away from Baguio. *Now is my chance.* I got up and pulled my bag over my shoulder.

"Um, excuse me, sir," I addressed the bus conductor. He stood outside the bus door watching as passengers got off. "I need to go back to Baguio." The poor bus conductor looked confused as I spoke to him in English. I could have spoken to him in my really bad Tagalog, the main Filipino language, but I was flustered and scared. I couldn't waste precious energy stumbling through unfamiliar words.

"Ah, ma'am, dis bus go to Manila."

"I know, but I need to get on a bus to Baguio. Is there a bus going back that way? I can't breathe. I need to go back to Baguio. Please!" I was trying really hard not to cry in front of him.

"Baguio, ma'am?" Flustered at having to speak in English, he called over the driver instead. "Dis Americana wants to go Baguio," he repeated to his co-worker. They discussed the options. I kept repeating that I was struggling to breathe.

"Ma'am," the driver said finally. "Dere is a bus dat will come in ten minutes dat take you to Baguio. You want to wait?"

"Yes!" I exclaimed and then thanked them both. Ten minutes later the kind conductor happily transferred me to my new bus, and I returned to the city where I should have stayed in the first place. Pink light rose over the peaks of the familiar mountains and hills as we neared the city limits. Once I was close enough to the city central, I exited the bus and caught a taxi straightaway to the nearest hospital. I walked into the ER clutching my blue-striped bag, nervous for what would happen next, and I was told to wait on a nearby vacant bed until a nurse could come.

I was 6,695 miles from home, in a hospital, all alone. What was I doing here? What had been running through my mind when I thought it would be a great idea to live in the Philippines? And by myself nonetheless. I told myself it would be no big deal. *I'm half Filipino—it'll be a breeze. It doesn't matter that I never grew up*

*with Filipino culture or learned more than two words in a Filipino language.*
*I'll be just fine. It will be my new home, and I'll be welcomed with open*
*arms like I'd been born there.*

It had been over three years ago, at a coffee shop in downtown Forest Grove, Oregon, that a conversation had planted the seeds, setting events into motion that eventually brought me to where I am today.

"Why don't you just join the Peace Corps?" my friend had asked me from across the table.

"What? Me? Join the Peace Corps?" I dismissed the idea at once.

"You want to live abroad, don't you?" he asked.

"Yes."

"You want to volunteer, right?"

"Yes, I need to do something different. I want to travel the world. Make a difference somewhere."

My friend smiled at this and paused for a moment. "You should join the Peace Corps."

I stared at him. *What a crazy idea.*

A month later I applied.

The letter bearing the Peace Corps logo arrived in the mail one fresh April morning. I had prepared myself to accept whatever country was offered (please God, NOT anywhere cold, like Mongolia!!!) and fully expected to get sent somewhere I had barely heard of, like Kazakhstan.

"Congratulations," it began. "You have been selected to serve as a Peace Corps Volunteer in the Philippines."

*The Philippines?!* I fell on my bed in dreamy bliss. Of all the countries I could have been assigned to I had somehow received the Philippines post—the country of my dad's birth. I'm half Filipino but was raised in an American household and never really experienced much Filipino culture growing up. Now in my twenties, those missing pieces of a culture I had never come to know or fully understand resurfaced in my exploration for self-identity. Was I Filipino because my skin was dark and I had a "squashed nose?" Was I American because I liked craft beer and made grilled cheese sandwiches for dinner? What did it mean to be Filipino or even Filipino American?

But now, with my induction into the Peace Corps, my quest for self-identity had arrived at my front door, literally, in the form of a thick government-issued envelope. I had embraced this new journey of identity, adventure, and service with open arms. This was my dream, I reminded myself. I had rejoiced in the fact that I would finally be able to live in the country of my dad's birth and learn about a culture I had always longed to know. I had hoped that the Philippines would be a new home to me—not just for the two years of my service contract, but for a lifetime. I had expected to feel immediately at home. But as I lay there waiting on the crackly mattress of the cold ER bed, alone, tired, dispirited, and weak in the lungs, I felt as far away from home as physically possible. *This isn't what I wanted.* Tears of nervousness and exhaustion dripped down my face and I wiped them away with my sleeve as I stared up at the printed letters "St. Louis Hospital" stenciled on the curtain. *This isn't what I wanted at all!*

## 2

## WELCOME TO THE PHILIPPINES

*July, 2011. Two years earlier.*

"Hey! Hey, Americana!"

I turned around and saw two skinny men lounging near a motorized bike with a sidecar for carrying passengers. Locals called these trikes. "Hey, Americana! Where you going?" shouted the taller man again.

"I'm just going to my house."

"I take you dere." He gestured for me to get into the trike.

"How much?"

"Twenty pesos only, eh."

"What? Twenty pesos? That's too much." I faked walking away.

"OK, OK! Ten pesos. Only because you are so beautiful," he added with a grin, flashing a row of half-missing teeth.

"Flattering," I muttered to myself. I boarded the trike while he gleefully jumped onto his bike seat, gunning the motor until it roared to life.

"How long you stay here in da Pilippines?" he asked as we bumbled along the road.

"I've been here a month already, but I'll be staying for two years."

"Two years! Wow, so long."

"I'm a volunteer, so I'm living here, *kuya*." Kuya translates as older brother and is a term of respect for males used even with strangers.

"Bolunteer! Wow, dat is so nice. How much your pay?"

"Nothing, kuya. It's volunteer work only."

"No money? Wow!"

The breeze hit my face as I leaned back in the plastic seat of the trike, welcoming the break from the continuous shroud of warm, sticky moisture. Arm in arm, two school girls in blue checkered uniforms gazed up at me as I flew by.

"So, you are Americana, no?" the driver asked.

"Yes, American."

"But you're Pilipino? You look Pilipino."

"Yes, my dad is Filipino."

"And you know how to speak Tagalog?"

"Only a little," I replied.

"Ah, well, you will have to learn how to speak Tagalog."

"Yes, kuya."

The trike rattled as we passed over a narrow bridge. A group of naked boys splashed in the shallow creek below, laughing and shouting. On the road ahead, a *taho* man shouldering a long bamboo pole with metal buckets on both ends made room for us to pass. He nodded at me with curious eyes and then continued on his way.

"Tahooooooo! Tahooooo!" he called out. The sweet pudding-like dessert he was selling was drizzled with caramel syrup and could be slurped through a large straw. From dawn until nightfall, the taho men wandered the town roads selling taho for only ten pesos a cup.

"So, you have boyfriend in America?" the driver shouted above the racket.

"No."

"You want Pilipino boyfriend?"

"Kuya, I'm not looking for a boyfriend."

"No? Why not? You don't want to get married?"

"Not right now."

"What age you want to get married?"

*What age?* "Kuya, I'll get married when I find the right person."

"Can I hab your number? You call me anytime to gib you rides."

I tried to hide my laugh. "No thanks, kuya. I don't have a cell phone." I stuffed my cheap phone farther into my jeans pocket. "Just over there, kuya. That house there." I pointed, and he pulled into the gravel driveway. I handed him a ten-peso coin. "Thanks, kuya!"

"Dank you, Americana! And welcome to da Pilippines!" he added with his broad, half-toothed smile before he puttered away.

Welcome to the Philippines. I smiled at his words, at that simple phrase. Welcome to the Philippines—the land of obnoxious roosters, flip-flops, and houses that smelled eternally of cooked rice, fish sauce, and laundry. My mind functioned slowly sometimes, working on overdrive to sort out the imagery it encountered, categorize it, and make sense of it. Or maybe it was just the heat. I couldn't be sure. Everything around me here had a distinct voice, smell, taste, or movement that heightened my senses. There was the low sizzle and pop of hot oil as street vendors stirred caramelized bananas in a giant wok. The undulating line of endless black ants, greedy for bits of forgotten food on the counter. Lush mangoes. Sweet green *dalandan* citrus. Vegetables piled high in stalls of the open-air market. Mangy, stray kittens curled up in balls of fluff, napping in patches of shade. Welcome to the Philippines.

As I crossed the gravel driveway, I had to maneuver my way through clotheslines of T-shirts and underwear hanging across the porch. "Helloooo!" I called through the screen door while I shuffled from street flip-flops to my pink house flip-flops.

"Debs, let's eat!" a voice called from within.

Just one month ago I entered this house for the first time after my host dad picked me up at the community center in Olongapo City. I had stood huddled with a flock of newbie Peace Corps trainees who were clustered in the center of the outdoor basketball court, pretending we weren't nervous. One by one we were matched up with a host family we'd be staying with for the next three months while we completed our Peace Corps training.

"Are you Pilipino?" my host dad asked, peering at me for the first time.

"Yes, part."

"Ah! I knew it! I says to myself, 'She must be Pilipino. She has da nose and da face of a Pilipino.'" And with that we walked to his brown, stained pickup truck with no working seat belts and a back window forever stuck at the halfway position. After hoisting my guitar and oversized suitcase into the truck bed, Host Dad got in and drove us through town. We passed restaurants and cafés with their names printed on signboards advertising cell phone services or Coke. A turquoise-colored karaoke bar up on the left, then a line of cement houses with corrugated roofs.

"Have you eaten yet?" Host Dad asked as we pulled up to the house.

For most of my life, the Philippines had always been that mysterious country from whence my Filipino aunties and uncles sent us ambitiously taped boxes of fluorescent souvenir T-shirts, banana chips, and weird milk candies. *What was the Philippines really like?* Now, here I stood, about to meet my host family for the first time, ready to learn what this Filipino culture thing was all about.

"Krispy Kreme?" my host brother asked as he shoved a paper box under my nose. Inside their dim living room with peeling, mint green walls, Harry Truman, my new host brother, offered me a donut. "You want?" he asked again as he held the box up to me.

*Really? The first snack they offer me is a donut from the US?*

"Wow...thank you, Harry. Mmm, sugar." Donut still in hand, I stood there, unsure of what to do. Host Dad and Harry Truman looked back at me. Little serving bowls filled with mystery dishes sat on the kitchen table next to us. I took a bite of donut. Harry Truman smiled. He was slightly chubby, and his large eyes bulged in a jolly sort of way. I smiled back.

"She's Pilipino." Host Dad pointed in my direction.

"Part," I added.

"Oh! So you must know how to speak Tagalog!" Harry Truman said.

"Only a few words." I devoured the last of the donut, trying to think of something to say.

"Let's eat, De-BOR-ah!" Harry Truman enunciated, inviting me to the table for lunch.

"Let's eat!" Host Dad handed me the large bowl of rice.

Welcome to the Philippines.

## 3

# HAVE YOU EATEN YET?

On the first night of sleeping at my host family's house, I was woken up at one thirty in the morning by a tickle on my arm. Instinct told me to slap my skin, but instead of swatting a tiny mosquito, my hand touched something different. A large creature squirmed underneath my sweaty palm. With a scream and mad flinging of arms, I catapulted the unknown thing across the room. Heart beating and blood pumping, I peered into the darkness searching for what I had killed. I saw nothing. I grabbed a flashlight and scanned the floor with my beam of light. Nothing.

And then I saw it. A quick shadow skittered across the floor. My flashlight shook. *What is it? A gecko?* They were harmless creatures and not too scary. *Please God, let it be a gecko!*

It darted across the floor again, and I saw a shape that resembled a cockroach. Wide awake, adrenaline racing through my veins, I couldn't sleep until that hideous thing lay dead. I turned off the fan so I could hear better and waited, poised with one hand holding the flashlight, the other hand armed with a flip-flop. The absence of the whirring fan made me sweat in the silence.

Suddenly the thing came at me, hurtling across the linoleum. I slammed my flip-flop down hard, but it escaped under a loose flap in the floor so I smashed my fist on the torn linoleum where it hid. After a few more hits for good measure, I lifted the flap and triumphantly uncovered a dead bug.

After momentary relief, I scanned the room again and saw two more skitter and hide as my light reached the far corners of the room. The hunt was on—no more sleeping. Tiptoeing around, I began precariously moving items, checking behind bags, language books, and suitcases, looking for them. One darted away as I moved a medical kit box. SLAM! WHACK! One more down. More searching.

I couldn't find them, but I could hear something—an awful, high-pitched, screeching. I sat there, crouched on my bed, too scared to close my eyes. *How am I supposed to sleep? Should I leave the light on?* Frantic texts to my Peace Corps leader were in vain.

I had been given a mosquito net earlier that day, but I hadn't had time to ask my host family how to set it up. I tore the plastic packaging off and tucked it around my mattress, covering myself in a sea of gauzy, green netting. Claustrophobic but safe, I lay down to go to sleep again. I could still hear screeching sounds coming from underneath my portable closet, but as I lay on my bed in safety, I smiled an evil smile.

*Screech on little bug, screech on. Little do you know I am plotting your demise. This girl's got a shoe, and she's not afraid to use it.*

"No, dat's not a cockroach. Dat's an *ipis*," Harry Truman told me the next morning. "Be careful. They can bite."

*Thanks for the advice, Kuya Harry. Thanks.*

I felt relieved that it hadn't been a cockroach, that is until I showed the picture to my Peace Corps leader who explained that in Tagalog an ipis *is* a cockroach.

~~~

In our first Peace Corps training class, the instructor conducted a culture-processing exercise where we were asked to draw a picture of the first day we spent with our host family. Furiously scribbling with my marker, I began drawing animated stick figures, floor mattresses, cockroaches, and seatless toilets. They were soon scattered across my paper, depicting a scene of chaos. Each stick figure represented the host family members I had met.

"Tagalog *lang*. Only Tagalog," said stick-figure Host Dad sternly in his little dialogue bubble. While fluent in English himself, Host Dad explained that speaking only Tagalog in the house would help me learn faster. As the proud host of an American, he took his duty seriously. During our first lunch, he instructed me, "If you don't understand something, you just ask." *Strict dad, I see. OK, I can do this…right?*

Harry Truman was my kuya, or older brother. At first I wondered about his name, but apparently, naming children after famous people was very popular in the Philippines. "I teach you!" stick-figure Kuya Harry said on my paper of chaos. He had reassured me that he would help me learn Tagalog words by the end of my stay.

My host mom, through her generosity and kindness, offered to buy me my favorite foods to help me feel more at home. In my drawing, her bubble read, "I buy you apples!" She was a nice balance to Host Dad's strict ways.

The stick-figure of Jessica, the baby of my host family, just giggled away, unable to speak yet.

There was a *lola*, or grandma of the house (*lolo* is the word for grandpa). Painfully shy, she hardly ever spoke to me directly. In my drawing I gave Shy Lola a blushing smile.

I managed to write one Tagalog word: *kain*. Actually, I wrote, "Kain! Kain! Kain!" which means, "Eat! Eat! Eat!" They said that to me a lot the first day. Apparently, I had learned some Tagalog after all thanks to Strict Dad's methods.

Also pictured on my paper of chaos was the floor mattress where I slept, and I included mysterious puddles in the bathroom adjacent to a ceramic toilet bowl. In the Philippines, a bathroom was called a "CR" which stood for "Comfort Room." However, in my host family's CR, there was no sink and the toilet had no seat. No seat. No sink. No toilet paper. On my paper of chaos, stick-figure Deborah had multiple question marks around her.

*So much for being a "comfort room!" Why is there no toilet seat? Am I supposed to just sit on the porcelain rim? How do I wipe myself? What is that ladle thingy and bucket of water next to the toilet used for?*

I eventually learned that the large bucket and ladle were for bathing as well as to pour water down the toilet in order to create a suction to flush it down. I think they also used the ladle and water for wiping, but I could never be sure. I immediately started bringing my own toilet paper and plastic bag each time I used the CR. I'd put the used toilet paper in the bag and then throw it away in the kitchen where I would also wash my hands. My host family must have thought I was weird for my bathroom routine. But I was thinking the same thing about them.

~~~

For our first three months in the country, my fellow Peace Corps volunteers and I underwent an intense training period. Our schedule kept us in constant motion with language and technical skill training courses from eight o'clock in the morning to five o'clock at night, Monday through Friday. Evenings were spent studying Tagalog, tutoring local kids at the nearby Social Development Center, or hanging out with our host families. On Saturdays we worked with the *barangay* officials, a local governing unit, on various community projects. Sundays were our free day. Free days meant I had time to do laundry, catch up on emails using the local McDonald's Wi-Fi, explore Olongapo City, hang out with my host family, and bury myself in more language study. Speak only in Tagalog, I could hear Strict Dad echoing inside my head.

Every afternoon when I returned home from Peace Corps training, I'd take out my language books to study in the main family room while Host Mom and Shy Lola prepared food for dinner. Kuya Harry would get home just before dinnertime, and I'd practice speaking Tagalog with him.

Upon first being welcomed into their home, I had given my host family a deck of UNO cards as a *pasalubong*, a souvenir gift from abroad. They loved the gift, and Kuya Harry and I would often play, using the colors and numbers as a way to practice our language skills. I would have to state the type of card in Tagalog, and he would have to say it in English.

"*Pula dalawa*," I said as I placed a red number-two card on the pile.

"Yellow two," Kuya Harry said as he put his card down.

Besides colors and numbers, Kuya Harry taught me the words for reverse (*balik*), draw four (*kuha apat*), and cheater (*madaya*). Card games were one of my favorite things to do with Kuya Harry because he always taught me new words for every little thing. A natural tutor, he made the frustrating process of language learning an enjoyable activity.

One evening, as Host Mom and Shy Lola cooked dinner, Strict Dad and Kuya Harry conversed together, pointing in my direction. I heard the word *kanta* used several times. Finally, they asked me if I was interested in singing.

"Singing? Where?"

They gestured outside.

Really helpful, I thought to myself. "Where?" I asked them again.

They pointed again and spoke more Tagalog that I didn't understand. *Right.* I decided to follow instead.

We walked a block down the road and entered a street-side dining canteen. Kuya Harry nodded for me to sit down at a green plastic table with a checkered plastic tablecloth. Strict Dad motioned to the waitress who brought over three San Miguel Light beers, a bowl of garlic peanuts, and a beat-up plastic karaoke book. It dawned on me that I had become a part of a pre-dinner karaoke session, or *videoke* as Filipinos liked to call it.

We spent the next few hours singing into a cheap, tin-sounding microphone, belting out Creed, Avril Lavigne, and Bon Jovi over a few rounds of beers. Local Filipino men sat around in weathered mint green plastic chairs watching those who sang. They boisterously cheered whenever anyone would hit a high note or holler into the mic like a diva.

"More! More! More!" they'd chant, falling into easy laughter and gaiety.

With only empty peanut shells left in the bowl, we exited the canteen and walked back out into the night, strains of off-tune Miley Cyrus still reaching our ears. I would soon become accustomed to the familiar sound of videoke—whether it was while shopping in the market, echoing down the valley of my neighborhood, or drifting out of some bar window at nine o'clock in the morning. Filipinos loved their videoke.

~~~

Early mornings in Olongapo were the only part of the day when I didn't have sweat collecting on my body. The air still felt cool and refreshing, albeit with a slight scent of pollution and exhaust, which constantly lingered over the national highway just outside my house. Having heard stories from previous volunteers about women gaining weight while serving abroad, I committed to staying active and exercising whenever I could. I decided to take advantage of the cool mornings and developed a routine of running all the way up to the top of the highway to a large statue called the *Kalapati*, The Dove Monument. It was gruesome run, but rewarding for its rigor. If I arose before six, I could catch a glimpse of sunrise beyond a cluster of patched, sagging houses and overgrown trees. A pink sky greeted me as I jogged up the steep hill, trucks and jeepneys speeding by, passengers staring at me like I was crazy. Perhaps I was a little crazy, even for an American.

"Where are you going?" a random man called out as I jogged past. He stared at me from his front doorstep.

"*Diyan lang*. Just there," I called back with my "cheerful volunteer" voice. I had just learned how to respond with that expression in language class the other day. "Just there" was a vague but friendly answer.

Surprised at my response in Tagalog, he laughed. "See you again!"

I smiled back and continued my run.

Returning home with sweat dripping off me like I had just been out in a rainstorm always sent my host family into a shocked, excited state. Each time they reacted with the same face of surprise and disbelief.

"You ran to Kalapati again?!" Kuya Harry asked incredulously.

"She's strong. She could be in the army," Strict Dad declared.

"She's wet!" Shy Lola commented.

"She ran *up* a hill!" Host Mom exclaimed.

After my Kalapati run, I would fill the plastic blue bucket in the bathroom, take the ladle, and pour cold water over my head.

"You must not take a cold bath after exercise," Filipinos warned me. "You will get *pasma!*" Apparently, pasma was a strange folk illness that would make your hands shake. *Pasma? Meh.* Cold bucket "showers" were welcome, especially on days when the oppressive heat and humidity did everything in their power to melt you to the core. Sometimes even minutes after taking a bucket bath, I'd sit in my room with beads of sweat running down my spine and want to go right back into the CR and do it again.

~~~

"*Kumusta ang hapon mo?* How was your afternoon?" Host Mom asked me as I returned home one day after training class. She and Shy Lola were sitting at the kitchen table cutting up vegetables for dinner.

"*Mabuti.* Good," I sputtered back in response.

"Wow, *magaling ang Tagalog mo!*"

"What?"

"*Magaling.* Very good. Your Tagalog is getting good."

"Ha, maybe one day."

"Yes, you just practice with your Kuya Harry. He'll tutor you." She pushed a bowl of fried bananas toward me. "*Kain na*, Debs. Let's eat now. Kain na!"

Kain na. "Eat now" embodies the most important thing you could ever say to someone in the Philippines. Sharing a meal means generosity, kinship, connection. To refuse such a gesture would be incomprehensible. I discovered that eating food meant navigating a tricky dance. Follow the correct steps, and no one's toes would get stepped on.

"Kain! Kain! Eat! Eat!" my family members would say earnestly as they passed dishes of savory food in my direction. Rice, pork, vegetables. I'd serve myself a portion of each, but not so much as to make me full. My plate would soon be empty and the dance would continue.

"Kain! Kain!" I would hear muttered again.

I'd nod and scoop more on my plate. Not quite full yet.

"I'm full," I'd say casually, pretending I was finished.

"Kain! Kain!" Kuya Harry would insist.

"OK." More food would go on my plate. While very delicious, I'd remind myself to eat slower. Not quite full yet.

"Kain! Kain!" Host Mom would tell me.

"I'm full."

"Kain! Kain!" Shy Lola would gesture.

"OK," I would respond with a smile and scoop food for the last time, my stomach having finally reached its maximum limit.

"Kain! Kain!"

"I'm full!" I'd say with more gusto. I'd rub my tummy. "*Busog.* Full."

They'd smile, proud that they had made me eat lots of food. I would smile too. It was just a dance.

Every volunteer had their own way of dealing with cultural issues, especially when it came to food. Sometimes I'd fake feeling sick or complain that I had diarrhea and that food was not going to help the situation. Usually though I opted for the I'll-eat-it-soon method, which I discovered worked well for avoiding food.

"Debs, your morning snack is ready!"

"But I just ate breakfast."

"Yeah, and now it's snack time! Kain na!"

"OK, I'm coming."

An hour later. "Debs, aren't you going to eat your snack? Kain na!"

"Oh yes, I'll eat it soon."

Two hours later. "Debs, your snack is still there. Don't forget to eat, *hah.*"

"Ok, I'll get it soon…"

In the Philippines, the ability to feed your family equated wealth. The fatter you looked, the more money you had. I often noticed wealthy families who, toting McDonald's fries and sundaes in one hand and Krispy Kremes in the other, were envied for their robust figures. Families who hosted volunteers welcomed their guests by feeding them. If the honored guest became bigger during their stay, they could show off their fat guest to their community. "You look so fat today!" and "Wow, chubby chubby!" were considered compliments.

Food is their language of love. No matter where in the world you meet a Filipino, they will inevitably offer you food as a welcome gesture. I can still remember from my childhood that every time our family visited my dad's parents, my *lolo* and *lola*, we would be offered food by my lola immediately upon our arrival.

"Have you eaten yet? You hungry?" she would ask.

"Oh, we actually just ate…"

"Here, you eat more food, hah," she'd say as she dished out rice and soup.

I usually ate what she offered—unless it was fish head soup. I never ate that. It wasn't the pearl white eyeballs floating in the broth that put me off. OK, maybe they *did* put me off. I actually didn't eat fish at all.

I hated eating fish as a kid, and when I had to, I'd force it down, covered in mayonnaise to mask the offensive taste. When I found out I was assigned to the Philippines, a country of over seven thousand islands, where seafood was a main part of the daily diet, I knew I'd be in trouble. Even in America, people gave me flak for not eating seafood.

"Why don't you like it?" they'd ask in astonished tones.

"I don't know. I just don't. It makes me nauseated."

"It's probably because you just haven't had seafood that's been cooked well."

"No. It literally makes me sick to my stomach."

"Maybe you're just not used to it. If you ate it more often, you might like it."

"If I eat one bite, I'm nauseated for the next few hours. Why would I want to eat it more often?!"

"Have you tried mackerel?"

If Americans could give me such anguish about what I liked and didn't like to eat, how much more would Filipinos react when they heard I didn't like a main staple in many of their dishes? So I came up with a plan. I began telling people that I was allergic to all fish and seafood. I even learned how to say it in Tagalog within my first few weeks in country. *May alergy ako sa isda.* I am allergic to fish.

"I can't eat it," I'd say with a look of tearful regret. "I'm allergic to fish." Then I'd mimic a sad face for extra effect.

At first people reacted with surprise, but they accepted that I could not eat anything with fish or seafood in it, including a dried, smoked fish called *tuyo*, and *bagoong*, which is a very pungent and purple shrimp paste. Fortunately, it turned out there were plenty of Filipinos who had allergies to certain types of fish or seafood. In fact, I learned that my lolo and my uncle both had allergies to shrimp and crab. I was not alone.

So while my fellow volunteers ate their whole fried fish for dinner—head, tail, and eyeballs still intact—I'd happily munch away at my pork *adobo*. Even though I'd still get comments from Filipinos that I was missing out on half my life because I couldn't enjoy fish, I was perfectly content with my choice.

Knowing how much food was an important part of building relationships, I decided one day to cook some American food for my host family. I told them that I'd be in charge of dinner that night. I planned to make tacos. They got excited.

"Yay! Tacos!" they exclaimed. Then they asked, "What are tacos?"

I found flour tortillas and Doritos corn chips at the American import store in Subic Bay, just a twenty-minute jeepney ride from the city, and I bought ground meat and fresh vegetables in the Olongapo open-air market. I carried everything home with me and got right to work chopping onions, garlic, and tomatoes. Kuya Harry watched me like I was preparing a gourmet meal.

"What are you going to do with that? What are the tor-till-as for?"

When all the food lay ready on the table, I called everyone over. They took one look at my guacamole and winced.

"What's that?! Is that avocado with *onions*?"

"Yes. And garlic and salt," I replied.

Their skeptical looks didn't dissuade me. I had already learned that in the Philippines, avocados were eaten with milk and sugar. Combining salt and garlic with avocados equated adding salt and garlic to cupcake frosting. Not very appealing.

"It's good. I promise."

They tried the guacamole and, while they admitted it was strange, they liked it. They especially enjoyed the tacos.

"We should make this for Christmas," Host Mom told Strict Dad excitedly.

"Kain na!" I urged everyone.

4

# SMOKEY MOUNTAIN

After several weeks into our Peace Corps training program, my fellow trainees and I gathered in Manila for a street immersion experience. The leaders designed the trip in order to acquaint us with some of the more difficult parts of the Philippines—poverty stricken areas, orphanages, street kids, human trafficking, and inner-city social service centers. During one of our first days, we drove to a place in Manila called Smokey Mountain.

Three vans filled with Peace Corps trainees pulled into a rutted, muddy driveway. The slippery, clay-like substance made a squelching sound as I stepped onto the ground. The sign at the entrance read "Smokey Mountain – Field of Dreams." From a distance, Smokey Mountain looked like a real mountain—a steep incline of rock, soil, and greenery. However, as we drew closer and began our walk up the narrow trail, it was evident that it was made of trash. Compacted trash. Bits of broken glass, shoes, plastic bags, and a hairbrush were all embedded on the path we tread. *Field of dreams?*

Smokey Mountain used to serve as an enormous landfill where thousands of people made their homes and picked through the trash for anything of value to sell. It eventually became an international embarrassment for the Philippines, a symbol of Manila's poverty and slums, and was closed down in 1995. Afterwards, the government implemented a public housing project for the residents near the site, however, with no source of income, many moved to another dumping site called Payatas—often referred to as the second Smokey Mountain.

As our guide led us up the mountain, we walked past a few houses that dotted the strange terrain—houses consisting of cardboard, tarp, metal scraps, and other miscellaneous materials. A naked boy sat in a red bucket of water outside his home and watched our group with wide, brown, glossy eyes as we passed by.

At the top of the mountain, I took in Manila's skyline off in the distance. I stood overlooking what was once the home and livelihood of thousands of people. It was difficult for me to process everything I had seen and learned so far. *How can the world be like this? Why does it have to be like this?*

As we began our descent, we encountered a few of the remaining residents on the mountain. Several men lounged outside their homes, smiling and nodding as we walked by. A woman dressed in a dusty tank top and shorts carried two stained brown bottles for holding water. Her daughter skipped ahead, playfully humming to herself.

Back in the vans, we headed to our next stop, and I stared out the window in withdrawn silence. Our next destination was the Payatas dumpsite which has a huge scavenger population despite the dangerous conditions caused by the large, unstable mounds of trash and refuse. I learned that in 2000, a landslide at Payatas killed over two hundred people, and left more than three hundred missing persons still buried beneath the trash. I felt shocked and horrified at this piece of news, trying to imagine what it would have been like for the families that had been present during that time.

As we entered the site, makeshift buildings and houses lined both sides of the road. Similar to the previous landfill, these houses consisted of an eclectic assortment of junk—corrugated metal, cardboard, a tent, fabric, wood, and tires. Many residents stared at us as we drove through, but most just smiled and waved.

Once outside the van, I ventured through trash and mud over to a long stretch of road. Around the fence, I observed a line of huts covered in a haze of thick, black smoke.

"Those are buildings where people make charcoal by burning pieces of wood," I heard someone mention. Smoke drifted in our direction, and I pulled my shirt over my mouth to breathe. A few feet away, three barefoot kids walked down the road unperturbed by the smell of smoke in the air. I watched a little girl clutching a stuffed animal. She ran to join her friends who were jumping and splashing in a mud puddle. They laughed and giggled.

Back in the van, I listened to the conversations of the other volunteers, nodding along to their sensory reactions and experiences. I stared out the window as we drove out of the dumpsite. People waved and smiled. My tears started to well up, but I held them back until we exited the area. Then they came, a slow dribble down my cheeks. I had participated in immersion trips before and had prepared myself for what I would encounter, but it didn't make it any easier to witness it. Until now, I had never seen destitute poverty on that level before.

Over the next week, I saw more situations and people that crushed me and tore at my heart. Our group made crafts with street kids, we visited several dingy social centers, and one evening in a sketchy part of town, a bar manager tried to charge me and some volunteers twice as much for our bill, refusing to let us leave until we paid the sum. Poverty in Manila, and in many parts of the Philippines, was not an easy thing to encounter. I took it all in, hoping that I could eventually process it in some meaningful way. Right now, I had too many questions without answers. On the trip back to Olongapo, freeways stretched out before me, but all I could see were the lines of dirty clothes hung up to dry, muddy and pitted roads, broken flip-flops half buried in the path, and the eyes of a wide-eyed toddler in a red bucket of water.

## 5

## NOSEBLEED

A lizard scampered across the wall in a pale shaft of moonlight. I watched its progress as I lounged, curled up on my mattress. I didn't have a bed in my room but instead slept on a faded pillow-like mattress on the floor. I had covered it in sheets and kept my mosquito net draped over it, tucking the ends underneath the mattress every night before I went to sleep. Unfortunately, this still did not prevent the cockroaches from getting at me, but there wasn't much else I could do. The only other furniture in the room was a portable covered closet and a small table with a chair.

As I lay on my pillow, the sound of heavy rain pelted on the roof, foreshadowing the imminent months of monsoon season. I always experienced a sense of awe whenever I listened to Philippine rain. It brought invigorating force and power. The thick tropical rain drenched everything in mere seconds. It pounded on corrugated metal roofs, threatening to beat houses into the mud. What was monsoon season without the squeaking of wet flip-flops sloshing through ankle-deep floodwaters? The rain would come all at once, and then there'd be nothing at all. It dribbled, showered; it ebbed and flowed. A patter of rain falling on the palms at night would soon turn to peeking sunlight and a chorus of birds singing alongside the roosters in the morning.

Rain. Roosters. Traffic. Breakfast cooking. People shouting, "Where are you going?" The sounds of daily life in the Philippines clung to me like sweat. Dogs howled at all hours of the night; chickens competed for equal amounts of noise. The gentle tinkle-tinkle of a bell announced the ice cream vendor. The clanging da-dang, da-dang, da-dang signaled the garbage truck passing through the neighborhood. Tanned and skinny men peddled the streets on their trikes selling a variety of goods, announcing their presence and the product they offered with loud, unintelligible calls.

"*Tahooooooooo*! *Taaaahooooooo*!!!" That was the taho man with his pudding dessert.

"*Mani*! *Mani*! *Manimanimanimanimani*!" Peanuts—a quick and easy snack.

"*Baluuuuut*! *Baluuuuuuuuut*!" Balut—the partially fertilized duck egg, which is boiled and eaten straight from the shell.

I knew without seeing it first that a jeepney—the main method of public transportation—was making its way up the hill. With a growling, sputtering engine, it lunged forward, belching out a cloud of black smoke. Then, tooting a merry, musical-sounding horn, it raced by leaving nothing but a choking haze of dirty exhaust. An iconic symbol of the Philippines, jeepneys were painted with bright colors, designs, or murals, and often adorned with tacky interior decor. They originated from old war jeeps. Just after World War II, the overabundance of American military jeeps were either given away or sold to Filipinos who converted them in order to drive passengers. The doors were placed at the back of the vehicle to allow passengers to quickly enter or exit at each stop. The first time I rode in a jeepney, I proudly handed the driver my fare with a cheery, "*Bayad po*! Fare, sir!" Then I sat back, one arm hanging out the window, and let the breeze whip my hair with warm Philippine air.

~~~

Strict Dad announced one evening that I would be number one in my language class. "You will," he insisted. The trainee who had stayed with them the previous year had been number two. He was hoping to get a number one this time around. I just smiled. His opinion didn't really matter to me. Why should I succumb to the pressure and high expectations of someone else? That was ridiculous. I mean, number one? Please. I was already busy trying to learn…well…everything. I had enough on my plate already. It's not like I would be a bad student in language class or anything. I probably wouldn't even come third. Then again, I didn't want to be second. The last volunteer had been second. That seemed so...un-epic. If I came second, Strict Dad would be disappointed. *I'd better get out those flashcards.*

When it came to language learning, I discovered that kids were my best friends. We automatically had many things in common.

"You can count to ten? Me too! High five!"

"Yup, I know how to say four different colors."

My limited ability to speak Tagalog in short constructed sentences was met with equal enthusiasm when spoken to children.

"*Masaya ang pusa.* The cat is happy."

"*Oo. Gusto niya ang mangga.* Yes. She likes mangoes."

At the market one day, I lingered near a produce stand admiring the bright colors of unfamiliar fruits.

"Hello, ma'am, sir," a woman addressed me. *Ma'am, sir?* This, I learned, was a common greeting of vendors, but I never quite figured out the reason.

"Um…*magkano ito*? How much is this?" I sputtered out, holding a cluster of baby bananas in my hand.

"*Sampu*. Ten."

I handed her a ten-peso coin. "*Americana ako*. I'm American," I added as an apology for my horrible pronunciation.

"Oh yes, ma'am, I know."

*How do they always know? It's my accent, isn't it?* I had, by then, come to the conclusion that my Filipino eyes, nose, and skin would only disguise me so far. Simply smiling was one thing. Noticing my American style of clothing provided a big clue. But opening my mouth gave me away every time. Especially that thick good ole American accent. I continually searched strangers' eyes for a hint of what they thought on the inside. I imagined their secret looks of scorn as soon as I turned my back.

How shameful, I'd imagine them thinking. A Filipino who can't speak her own language. I could picture the old lolos and lolas shaking their heads and clicking their tongues with a tisk-tisk.

Anyway, I'm American, I insisted to no one in particular. Why should I have to speak Tagalog perfectly?

After a while, it occurred to me that my American looks were even more obvious than I realized. Oftentimes while exploring, I attracted unwanted jeers from random store clerks or passing trike drivers. One day while passing through the market, I heard someone call out to me.

"Hey! Hey, Americana!"

I kept walking. I was getting tired of this kind of attention.

"Hey! Hey there! Hello, Americana!"

"Yes?" I said in resignation.

"Where are you going?

*Why do they always ask where I'm going?* "Just there," I responded.

"You are Americana?"

"Yeah."

"I love you!"

"Uhh…" Time to walk the other way.

Although shouts of "Hey, Americana" or "Hey, foreigner" usually sent a scowl to my face, I unwittingly found myself drawn to curious bystanders. Conversations with strangers filled me with a sense of pride, as if I had accomplished something productive. *Volunteer holds a conversation with a local Filipino!* I should have gotten a gold star.

Exploring the streets of Olongapo and meeting random people soon became my new hobby. As I wandered the stalls of the open-air market, I observed people going about their daily business. Elderly lolas gossiped together while eating rice cakes. Two men sat at ease, smoking and chuckling while their third companion remained fast asleep on a flimsy plastic chair. Street kids ran with dilapidated flip-flops, thrusting their palms out to passersby, demanding money with silent, pouting faces. A pregnant woman picked out dalandans and placed them on a scale for weighing. Two kilos. She gathered several more pieces. Her son held on to her baggy shirt with one fist, clutching a plastic bag with orange soda and a straw in the other.

Whenever I'd meander through downtown Olongapo, I would notice a lot of school kids walking around with buttons that read "Speak English to Me." The Department of Education expected that all children would learn English in the classroom. One day I tried talking to one of the button students.

"Where do you go to school?" I asked a high school girl while standing in line for the jeepney. She looked back at me in confusion.

"Where do you study?" Blank stare.

"Do you speak English?" I assumed from the fearful deer-in-the-headlight eyes that she didn't speak much English at all. I reverted to my broken Tagalog and tried to talk to her a little.

She still looked scared of me. I'm not sure that her button was helping her.

~~~

One afternoon, while shopping for snacks in a grocery store near the market, I heard a voice behind me.

"Where are you from?"

I turned around.

"You're not from around here, are you?" a store clerk said, standing next to the shelf of Chicharron ni Mang Juan chips and adobo-flavored Corn Nuts. *How do they always know?*

"*Taga America ako*. I'm from America," I told her in my thick American accent then continued my search for American peanut butter. The Filipino peanut butter I ate in the morning on occasion with *pandesal*, sweet Filipino rolls, was always mixed with sugar, and I was hoping for the good, American, salty tasting peanut butter. It had to be here somewhere. Another Peace Corps volunteer told me he had found some just the other day.

She leaned forward and peered at me. "But you're half Pilipino?"

"*Opo*. Yes."

"So! You know how to speak Tagalog!"

"Just a little." I shrugged my shoulders and looked away. *Now, where was that peanut butter? Why didn't the Philippines have good peanut butter?*

"So what are you doing here in da Pilippines?"

"I'm a volunteer."

"You married?"

"No."

"Why not? Do you have boyfriend?"

"No. No boyfriend."

"Do you want Pilipino boyfriend? I have cousins."

I politely declined then hurried off to find my peanut butter before she could ask me my age, where I lived, or how many kids I planned on having. I learned within a week of living in the Philippines that personal questions were normal, casual conversation starters. While to a foreigner these questions seemed intrusive and personal, to Filipinos it invited the chance to form relationships. In fact, every time I met someone for the first time, it always proceeded in the same way, with the conversation sounding something like this:

"So...you're American?"

"Yes, American."

"But, you're not Pilipino? You look Pilipino."

"Yes, I'm Filipino."

"So your mom is Pilipino?"

"No, actually my dad is Filipino."

"So you're half American, half Pilipino?"

"No, I'm full American." Confused faces always seemed to follow that remark.

"I'm *Filam*," I offered. Generally, the term Filam describes a Filipino American. At the time I didn't really refer to myself as Filipino American. I didn't fully understand what that term meant or assumed that it meant someone who was full Filipino but was born in the US. So when using Filam to describe myself, I always had to preface it by saying that I wasn't familiar with the culture and I didn't speak any Filipino languages.

"Oh, so you're not *pure American* then? What about your mother? Is she pure American?"

*Pure American?* I wondered at the term. *What did that even mean?*

Most Filipinos associated the term American with someone who had fair skin, blond hair, and blue eyes. Since I didn't fit that description, I caused a lot of confusion. And because I looked and had Filipino ancestry, it meant that I should speak at least one Filipino language.

"So you're Pilipino?" a school official asked me one day while a few volunteers and I toured the school facilities.

"Yes, my Dad is Filipino. He's from Iloilo."

"So you must speak Ilonggo," he said, referring to the dialect spoken by many in Iloilo and the surrounding provinces in the Visayan region.

"No."

"But then you speak Visayan?"

"Umm, no."

"But, of course, then you must know how to speak Tagalog."

"Just a little." Emphasis on the word *little*.

~~~

My famed "run to Kalapati" became a regular routine that I craved—needed—for more than just the exercise. It gave me a sense of freedom and independence. I was so accustomed to an independent lifestyle in the US that when I encountered the opposite in the Philippines it made me feel claustrophobic, like I didn't even have space to breathe. There were no places to just be by myself; people were everywhere. Host family members filled the house, constantly asking what I was doing, if I wanted to eat again, or telling me how to do something a certain way. Strangers on the street stared, asked awkward questions, or pestered me about where I was going.

"What are you doing?"

"Are you a Pilipino?"

"Americana! Hey, foreigner! Where are you going?"

"Don't forget to eat, Debs, so you will get fat."

Sometimes I could escape for a brief respite in the backyard when I did my laundry. The process took several hours, but I enjoyed the time to leisurely wash my things without someone asking me where I was going or what I was doing. My host family had an electric washer, so I used the garden hose to fill it up and then hit the button to wash for one cycle. When the timer clicked back to start, I'd open the drain and let the blue-green water seep out onto the cement slab, then it would cascade further on into the dirt and grass clumps. I'd plug the drain, fill the washer up again with hose water, and repeat for three or four cycles. I'd hang everything, underpants and bras included, up on the line. There's nothing like letting your underwear sway proudly in the breeze for all to see.

~~~

Two months into my training, I hit a wall. I did not want to encounter another cockroach. I wanted to punch the next person who asked me if I was American or why I didn't speak Tagalog. I was sick and tired of telling people where I was going. *Just there, OK?* I locked myself in my room and let my tears soak my pillow.

"Debs, your afternoon snack is still dere."

"Hey! Are you Pilipino?"

"Let's eat now!"

"You should learn to speak Tagalog."

"She should be in da army!"

"I want a number one."

"You're getting so chubby-chubby now."

"Why aren't you married yet?"

"Do you want a Pilipino husband?"

As I grew up, my dad's stories of the Philippines resembled fairy tales. Sometimes they involved encounters with *kalabaw* (water buffalo), eating sugar cane, or traveling to a relative's house on a donkey. I mean, seriously, riding a donkey to the next town over? People did things like that? But those stories were the closest connection I had to Filipino culture in an otherwise American household. As I grew older, I began to regret that I had somehow missed out on something I couldn't quite explain or define. Maybe I had never gotten the "Filipino American" experience—whatever that meant. My identity as a Filipino American had always felt ambiguous. It was definitely not something I felt I could claim as my own. Sure, I knew what *lumpia*—the Filipino version of an egg roll—tasted like. I had learned *tinikling*, a traditional Philippine dance, and I remembered loud parties at my relative's house where singing bad karaoke was just as important as the overflowing pot of white rice. But what did it mean to be Filipino? I couldn't answer that question.

As I lay with my face pressed on the damp pillow, I had to remind myself that I wanted this. I asked for this. But I couldn't help thinking of the random Filipinos I'd met on the street, how they laughed or giggled at my accent and inability to speak Tagalog. "But you're Pilipino, right? And you don't speak Tagalog?" *No! I didn't ask for this!*

I ran to Kalapati. I needed to breathe some fresh air.

"Where are you going?" the same man called out to me from his front doorstep as I pounded the hill. I pretended not to hear. I didn't smile back.

My legs carried me with a steady, rhythmic motion; blurry trees whisked by in my periphery. Cockroaches, personal questions, my underwear hung up on the line for all to see. I was determined to survive. *I didn't know how to speak Tagalog? So what!* What about the blushing girl at the bakery who couldn't stop laughing in embarrassment because of her poor English skills when speaking with Americans? What about the old men loitering on the street corner who laughed at themselves because they couldn't remember the right English words to say? They called it a "nosebleed"—something akin to a brain freeze in English.

"Ha, ha! I hab nosebleed," they chuckled, making fun of themselves. Laughter. That's how Filipinos dealt with stressful situations. Why couldn't I do the same?

~~~

"Wild card. Draw four cards, Kuya Harry!" I laughed in evil delight while he added more cards to his hand. "And I choose *berde*. Green." I slapped down a green nine card.

"Red nine." Kuya Harry put down a red six.

"Madaya! Cheater!" I laughed as I flung his card back at him. "Kuya, that's a six. *Anim*."

"Oops!" he laughed. "Here, a green five card."

"Kuya, how come you're so good at English?"

"Eh, I'm not good. English is so very hard. I get nosebleed. Especially when I meet your American friends."

"Oh, your English is good, Kuya! Tagalog is hard. I get Tagalog nosebleed all the time."

"Hah!" he chortled. "Dat's a good one! I will tell dat to my friend. An American has nosebleed! Dat's funny!"

I laughed, "Yup! A Filipino Americana with a nosebleed!"

Although I started to make a conscious effort to laugh at my inabilities in Filipino style, my struggles with cultural adjustment did not magically disappear. They lingered with me throughout my journey, sometimes forgotten, sometimes bubbling uncomfortably close to the surface. But I was learning to be patient. The next few years would clearly require a lot of patience out of me.

~~~

After three months spent in the exhaust-filled city of Olongapo, our training drew to a close, and I prepared for my departure to Manila for our official Peace Corps swearing-in ceremony. While I had just begun to get to know my host family and was sad to leave them, I was looking forward to my volunteer placement at a site where I'd be working at for the next two years. During the final week at my host family's house, Kuya Harry coached me on Tagalog, Strict Dad listened with satisfaction, and Shy Lola began speaking to me for the first time.

*Why is she just now speaking to me?* Usually she either made hand motions or got embarrassed and had another family member translate for her. I was used to interpreting hand signals from Shy Lola, similar to playing charades. Ooh, I know this one. Hanging? No, laundry! You mean the laundry is dry? Yes! I win. I'll go get my laundry. Maybe she overheard me practicing Tagalog with Kuya Harry, and she thought that I'd learned something. Maybe I *had* learned something.

The morning I left my host family's house for the last time, I said my final goodbyes. "Don't forget to send me a message when you get married so I can send you a gift," Host Mom told me as she gave me a hug. Kuya Harry helped me load my bags into the waiting van filled with other volunteers. As I waved goodbye, the van pulled out of the gravel driveway, turned onto the national highway, and we were off, speeding past the canteen with the karaoke machine, past the rows of houses with corrugated metal roofs, past the Kalapati statue, out of Olongapo City, and onto the next stage of our unknown journey.

## 6

## COUNTRY MUSIC, MOUNTAIN ROADS

I sat at the table looking attentive and interested as two Peace Corps staff members questioned me. They were in charge of placing me with the agency where I'd work for the entirety of my service. This assignment was something I had been eagerly awaiting.

"As we discussed before, I think you are going to be a perfect fit for the site I mentioned. You'll be working with youth programs and perhaps even be doing something with music." The Sector Manager grinned as he explained the details of the site. "I can't tell you where the site is located, but you'll find out as soon as we make our final decision."

Smiling jovially, the Site Manager asked me, "So, do you like vegetables?"

"Yeess…?" I replied with slow deliberation, not quite sure what he meant by the question and whether my answer would have repercussions.

"Good!" he smiled with a twinkle in his eye. "You'll be just fine!"

I was placed in Baguio City, often referred to as the salad bowl of the Philippines. It was located in Benguet province in the mountainous Cordillera region, and the surprisingly cool temperatures made it ideal for growing produce. Drivers traveling the Halsema Highway could see hundreds of vegetable terraces flowing down every mountain edge and incline. Jeepneys and open-bed trucks piled high with *kamote* (sweet potato), *ampalaya* (bitter gourd), and *pechay* (bok choy) rumbled along, making their way into Baguio to the enormous fresh market. Fresh vegetables and strawberries were the region's specialties. Any Filipino visiting Baguio would be reprimanded if they didn't bring back a box of fresh strawberries, or at least strawberry jam, as a *pasalubong* gift. Green beans and carrots bought directly from the Baguio market were somehow more appealing than those purchased from a market elsewhere. "Don't forget to buy me Baguio beans!" a mother might tell her son before he embarked on his trip north to the mountains.

I arrived in Baguio after a nine-hour bus ride that was supposed to be six, up the mountains in a torrential rainstorm. Carmelita, my soon-to-be co-worker, had accompanied me on the journey. When we finally arrived, she dropped me off at a house at the top of a long flight of stairs.

"Welcome, Debs!" my new host mom said as she greeted me with a hug. She walked me down the hall of her three-bedroom house and opened a door to reveal a Pepto-Bismol pink room. "Here is where you'll stay," she gestured. The room had pink walls, a pink closet, and a pink desk. Two windows revealed sunlight hitting the pine trees outside. The gentle sound of a creek nearby soothed my mind. Best of all, the room contained a real bed with a mattress. No more sleeping on the floor with the cockroaches. I felt like I had won the lottery.

When my host mom showed me the location of the CR, I noticed that the toilet had a real seat *and* it flushed. I would no longer have to pour a bucket of water down the toilet to create a suction for it to flush. Luxury. However, as I put my bags down in my room, it occurred to me that there was no room fan.

"You can call me Mama Ginny," my host mom said. "Just unpack your things and relax now."

I was standing in the CR brushing my teeth when I heard the handle rattle. The knob turned, and the door flew open. In walked a little boy who, without a second glance, pulled down his jeans and proceeded to pee in the toilet. Of course the only logical thing to do in that situation was to start a conversation. So I did.

"Oh...hi...who are you?"

"I'm Khurt. I'm watching SpongeBob and Mom said I can't watch it I have to eat but I want to watch SpongeBob because he's funny. I don't like to eat because Lola is making noodles but I don't like."

"Oh. Uh huh."

Later that day, Mama Ginny asked me if I had met Khurt yet. *Yes. Yes, I had.*

It turned out Khurt was only one of many kids who lived at the residence, a compound of four connected houses. His younger brother, Carlito, was an adorable three-year-old who always got the short end of the stick, at least whenever Khurt was around. Francyn, their older sister, had long, thick, curly hair and liked to come into my room, sit on my bed, and talk to me like a sister. She even referred to me as her *ate*, which means older sister. I soon found out that Francyn liked to sing, and we'd often jam together with my guitar while waiting for dinner to be ready.

One evening, Francyn and I lounged in my room staring at the ceiling. The coolness of the night helped clear my mind. I relaxed. No room fan was needed in Baguio, after all.

"So tell me more about this boy, Lucas," I teased her. Francyn squirmed and couldn't help but smile. I poked her. "Tell me!"

"OK, fine, Ate Debs. Well, he plays basketball. He is friends with my friend John."

"Is he *pogi*? Handsome?"

She blushed.

"Debs! Francyn! Let's eat now!" Mama Ginny called from the kitchen.

"Come on, let's eat. You can tell me all about him after dinner." I smiled and poked her again.

~~~

Life in Baguio was much different from Olongapo. Since it was up in the mountains, the weather was cool and comfortable. And instead of taking language classes and other courses, I finally got to start my volunteer work at a local school and community center. My commute Monday through Friday involved taking two jeepneys to the other side of the city to a neighborhood called Irisan. At first, the community center director sent someone each day to fetch me and take me to work. But after a few days, I convinced them that I could handle the jeepney ride on my own.

On one of my first days riding to work on my own, I felt like a kid heading to her first day of school. I climbed into the back of the jeepney and handed my eleven pesos to the jeepney kuya. "Pinesview," I said, telling him the name of my stop. I squeezed into a spot between two women on their way back from the market. They had plastic sacks full of vegetables clustered around their legs. One mother fed bite-sized cookies to her baby.

"Irisan! Irisan! Room for one more to Irisan!" the jeepney kuya called out. We needed another passenger before we could leave the station. A dark-skinned lolo stepped on and took the last spot at the end. The jeepney rumbled and snorted then rolled out of the terminal. I twisted in my seat to catch a view out the window behind me and watched the last of the city pass by until green spaces opened up on one side of the highway. The morning sun highlighted the subtle incline of the valleys and the large curves of the mountains in the distance. I inhaled, trying to catch a whiff of the pine trees clustered on the hill. I coughed. All I could smell was jeepney exhaust.

The jeepney followed the road around each mountain curve, and I kept watch out the opposite windows, trying to discern which highway curve was my stop. Two small turns, then one big one. Past the mini gas station. Past the field with banana trees. This was it.

"*Para*! Stop!" I called out to the driver. He shifted gears, put on the breaks, then pulled to the side of the road. "Excuse me," I repeated as I stooped to walk down the aisle past the other passengers, and stepped out the back door.

"Good morning!" I called out to Jay Ar who stood outside on gate duty.

"Good morning, Ate Debs!"

Most of my Filipino co-workers called me Ate or Ate Debs. It took me awhile to get the hang of new titles.

"Ate Debs, we're having a meeting tomorrow," Carmelita informed me.

"You can just call me Debs if you want."

"But you are older. That means you are my ate."

"Oh…OK then."

Things became even more confusing when I wasn't sure of someone's age.

"Hey, Ate Jocelyn, how are you?" I addressed another co-worker, Carmelita's sister.

"Ate Debs, I'm not your ate. You are older than me."

"Oh, right."

The organization where I worked operated an elementary school as well as community outreach programs for youth and families. The school building, painted with cheerful red, yellow, blue, and green, offset the gloominess of the cement block structure. "Speak in English" signs were tacked up on various doors and walls. Each morning, in accented staccato voices, the children would recite in unison, "Good, mor-ning, Tea-cher. It's, nice, to, see, you, a-gain." And then again after class was dismissed, "Good-bye, and, thank, you, Tea-cher. See, you, a-gain, to-mor-row."

I spent most of my days in the center's office, which I shared with Carmelita, Jocelyn, the center director, and later on, another volunteer from Australia. The office had large glass-slatted windows with a view of a sprawling hillside in the distance. Sometimes I could watch small outlines of people putting up laundry on the clothesline; other times I could see goats grazing away.

The Irisan neighborhood was just outside the main city, and so it had a more relaxed atmosphere. But the city of Baguio itself constituted a crammed collection of houses in overpopulated neighborhoods, pushing the city pollution and waste management problems to another level. Piles of burning trash left trails of gray smoke rivaled only by the haze of exhaust from jeepneys, cars, trucks, motorbikes, and taxis. It was no wonder that whenever I tried to go for a run, I'd come back wheezing or find black smears on my Kleenex.

Baguio's big-city conveniences came at the cost of overcrowded, urban areas where going against the flow on the main street, Session Road, was like fighting the rush of a monsoon flood. Even walking with the stream of pedestrian traffic meant skillfully passing old lolos and lolas walking too slow, distracted aunties walking too slow, groups of teenagers walking too slow—basically everyone in the Philippines walking too slow. And it wasn't just the people you had to plough through. Streets were like obstacle courses, which meant dodging vendor carts, men covertly trying to sell you knockoff brand sunglasses, and stout women balancing baskets of bananas on their heads like it was no big deal.

"Bananas! Bananas! Buy now!"

Dinky rolling carts managed by food vendors could be found in small pockets all over the city. Giant, rainbow-striped umbrellas, which shaded carts or tables, became an emblem of street food, a subconscious clue of something tasty for sale. Certain sections in downtown Baguio sold fresh, ready-to-eat fruit. Older women wrapped in shawls and wearing broad straw hats, squatted low to the ground, peeling and slicing fruit. *Suha* (pomelo), guava, pineapple, *santol* fruit, and mango slices served with purple bagoong shrimp paste. Yes, mangoes dipped in shrimp paste.

At night, metal grates used as barbecue grills nestled hot coals that glowed with spirit in the evening twilight. The kuyas and ates tended their fires with care, fanning the flames with pieces of cardboard, ashes flying into the air like softly falling snow. Liver chunks, intestines, and other unknown parts of an animal stood skewered and marinated, waiting to be cooked over the miniature flames. Vendors grilled fish stuffed with onions, garlic, and green peppers, then wrapped them in newspaper to be sold to a waiting crowd of hungry customers.

With its enticing vendors, stores, cafés, and bars, Baguio also had a way of sucking you dry of cash, forcing you onto a diet of packaged Pancit Canton instant noodles for a few weeks until the next payday. Instant noodles were only ten pesos a pack. As a Peace Corps volunteer, our allowance was meager and all too often when funds ran low I found myself eating the cheapest food available—instant noodles and rice. Sometimes, when cash dwindled to especially uncomfortable levels, I ate meals consisting of only rice. Fried garlic mixed with rice. Actually, eating garlic rice for dinner was not that bad, once in a while.

Despite the crowded and exhaust-filled streets, weather-beaten and dilapidated storefronts, which were typical of any Filipino city, there was something about living in Baguio that took a hold of me slowly over time. The city was a collection of families who had come from, or still lived in, the mountain province areas. Their traditions and way of life—quiet, dignified, hard-working, artistic, spiritual—personified the spirit of Baguio. You could immediately spot someone who came from out of town by the way they acted. Talking loud, sporting brand-name sneakers, wearing shorts and tank tops, and disobeying pedestrian "walk" signals all revealed non-Baguio people.

An overabundance of country bars also indicated that you were in a Cordillera mountain region. Yes, San Miguel beer and country music served up all night long. I never understood how that one specific music genre had infiltrated the entire mountainous region while bypassing the rest of the seven thousand plus Philippine islands. And yet the preference remained clear, Cordilleran people loved their country music. Sometimes when I close my eyes and think back, imagining an older native Igorot man, I picture a tanned face, worn and wrinkled like leather, a smooth black cowboy hat tipped just below the eyes, and a cheap cell phone scratching out country songs at full volume. Each time I journeyed through the mountains to other provinces, the vehicle always played country music, twanging out of the bus or van speakers.

The word Igorot means "people of the mountain." Unfortunately, there was a stigma associated with that name, and it referred to the Cordilleran mountain residents as monkeys who lived in trees. Filipinos from the lowland regions often used the term in a derogatory way, depicting the indigenous Igorots as stupid, living a backward way of life. However, in the few years before I arrived, there had been a new movement amongst Igorots to claim their name with pride. I often noticed people in the Cordillera provinces wearing shirts that read "Igorotak," which means "I am Igorot." Igorots were soft-spoken but full of pride and dignity for their way of life.

People-watching was one of my favorite things to do in Baguio. I once encountered an Igorot woman who clutched her basket of *sayote* leaves, the skin of her hands hardened with years of rough washing and housework. She was not hindered from doing her chores by the child slung over her shoulder wrapped in dark green and black weavings. Nor did the little one prevent her from ducking into a jeepney while carrying two large grocery bags of produce. There were plenty of women like her, ones with bursting pregnant bellies, carrying a baby on their back, shouldering bags from the market, and yet they still managed life with nonchalant ease. I watched women like that in awe. Strong, uncomplaining, hardworking.

Then there was the jeepney kuya, a younger Igorot man of the mountain provinces, who wore dirty jeans, a knockoff North Face jacket, and a woven plaid scarf draped around his neck. He always carried a colorful handwoven backpack or a Cordilleran basket on his broad shoulders. With long, black hair flipping back and forth in the breeze, he put a cigarette to his lips and gazed lost in thought toward the mountains in the distance, curls of smoke etched in the twilight.

There were so many beautiful places to visit in the Cordilleran mountain region. I could hop on a bus any free weekend and be on my way to some new adventure filled with hiking, caving, and roadside cafés serving room temperature meals, flies coming in for a landing every few seconds like an international airport. I hiked Mt. Timbak to visit the Kabayan

Mummy Burial Caves, Mount Cabuyao to view an aerial lookout of Baguio, and Mount Pulag—the third highest peak in the Philippines—to watch the sunrise over a sea of clouds. Every place I visited brought new excitement and adventure, and I could always count on a bumpy, curvy ride with country music blaring through twenty-year-old speakers.

Country music. Mountain roads. Plaid scarves. Colorful weavings. Backpacks. Swaddled babies. These are solidified in my memory as Cordilleran mountain life.

## 7

## A GREEN CURTAIN AND A PHOTOGRAPH

"I'll be taking you to visit some of the families from our school," my co-worker Ligaya told me. I called her Ma'am Ligaya out of respect and did the same with several other parents who volunteered at the school. Ma'am Ligaya had a genuine, unassuming nature and a gorgeous smile, which remained poised to break out in warm laughter at any moment. As we wandered the uneven gravel roads during these community visits, I loved listening to her tell stories as she clutched my arm in gentle familiarity.

"Let's go," she said, reaching out her arm.

We tread with care down a rocky dirt path and made our way to a house tucked behind a mass of tangled greenery and banana trees. At each of the community visits, I introduced myself as the new volunteer. Conversations followed—sometimes in Tagalog, sometimes Ilocano (one of the main Filipino languages spoken in this region)—and if I was lucky, in Taglish, a combination of Tagalog and English. I tried my best to follow along, watched hand gestures and facial expressions, sat in a continual state of bewilderment, but would always smile politely nonetheless.

I ducked under a few clotheslines, shirts and pants gently swaying in the breeze. Chickens puffed their feathers as they shuffled across the yard, and several scruffy dogs watched without moving, acknowledging our presence with a slight tilt of their heads. A woman greeted us with hushed tones, beckoning us through the doorway of her house, a structure consisting of corrugated metal walls and roof.

"Dis is Ma'am Deborah. She is our Peace Corps bolunteer. She is from America," Ma'am Ligaya told the woman in English for my benefit.

The woman smiled at me. "Have you eaten?" She grabbed a bag of pandesal sweet rolls and offered them to Ma'am Ligaya and me.

"Thank you, *po*." I selected a pandesal roll out of the bag. Po was a term of respect used in polite conversation. Call anyone po and you were in good shape, even if your Tagalog was horrible.

The mother's shyness wore off as she began to chat nonstop with us about her daily life. Her two toddlers, a son and daughter, clambered on and off her lap, fidgeting and fussing until she gave them some pandesal and peanut butter. She balanced her youngest son on one knee, pulling back his hands each time he tried to dip them into the peanut butter jar. A pot of rice on the stove whistled with excess steam, and she got up to turn down the heat.

Half an hour later, deeper into the conversion and now completely in Tagalog, the mother began tearing up. The volume of her voice increased. I stared at her toddler, still clutching the peanut butter jar. His hands were deep inside it now that his mother remained occupied with her story. I squinted in the dark at a pile of folded clothes. Next to it, a much larger pile of unfolded clothes. The woman cried harder. Ma'am Ligaya spoke sympathetic words. I looked on, helpless.

"What did she say, Ma'am Ligaya?" I asked once we were outside. The chickens cawed loudly as we passed by.

"Ah, her family is having troubles with da rent and bills. Her husband has only a small job. Dey have many expenses because of da school. Dey have five children, eh."

"Oh, I see."

"Let's go." Ma'am Ligaya took my arm, and we continued on.

We visited another family from the school who lived farther from the main road down a winding cement lane in a boarding house that rented out single rooms. I followed her into the building, and we climbed a steep wooden staircase leading to an ominous dark hallway. With my head bent down, I tried my best not to bump against the ceiling, which was not made for someone of even modest American height. As Ma'am Ligaya knocked on one of the doors, cries of an infant could be heard through the thin wooden walls.

The mother of the crying baby emerged from the doorway and signaled us to enter. One queen-sized bed and a small bench were the main pieces of furniture that occupied the tight space. Although I was certain Ma'am Ligaya had told me this woman had four kids, I wasn't convinced. It didn't look like enough space for even a husband and wife, let alone an entire family. I silently took stock of the objects in the room: stacks of folded clothes in lieu of closets, piles of various sized shoes, a gray mosquito net draped from the ceiling enclosing the mattress. My eyes drifted toward the window without a screen, just a simple green square of curtain scrunched off to one side.

I smiled at the petite woman with the baby resting on her hip. His cries still pierced the silence of the dark hallway. *How could anyone possibly live in this tight, claustrophobic room?* Ma'am Ligaya and the mother conversed in Ilocano. I fidgeted and stared intently at the green fabric scrunched to one side of the window. I heard the chickens babbling outside. When it came time for saying our goodbyes, I mustered out another smile and whispered a polite "thank you, po" before exiting the boarding house, past the shared kitchen and bathroom downstairs, out into the light of the open air.

After one of our home visits, I caught a glimpse of gorgeous, green-covered mountains behind the house. "Can I take picture?" I asked. Already, my English was becoming garbled as I unconsciously dropped articles for simplicity. The woman nodded but gestured for me to follow her behind the house. Her back cement porch offered a better shot of the entire landscape. The vast reaches of rolling, lush hills, the endless mountain ranges, and the unfading beauty left me stunned. I took a picture quickly and then shoved my camera away, suddenly feeling stupid. Taking a picture felt too awkward, like I had trespassed on someone's private life. The contrast of the scene—natural beauty and striking poverty all in one click of a camera aperture—unnerved me.

~~~

"And dis is my *bahay*, my home," Ma'am Ligaya gestured as we stepped past a metal door into a room with a dirt floor. She bought Coca-Cola and SkyFlakes Crackers at a neighbor's store, and then we sat down at her kitchen table to have morning *merienda*, a snack.

"You want coffee? I make you some."

"*Salamat, po.* Thank you, Ma'am Ligaya."

She smiled brightly, and I grinned back. It was contagious, that smile of hers. The past few weeks of home visits had been overwhelming, but Ma'am Ligaya always helped keep my spirits high. She remained hopeful for her community, and that was evidenced in the way she conducted herself. She showed up to community meetings on time, even when the rest of the community showed up on Filipino time, two hours later. She desired change and accepted the challenge of being the one to model it. Her leadership earned her respect in the community, but her genuine motherly love of others solidified it.

She brought over two mugs of coffee then handed me a banana bunch that had been sitting on her counter.

"Here, you eat dese bananas," she insisted. "Dey are from our tree outside."

"Yum! I love bananas. Thank you, po!"

## 8

## JOLLIBEE OR MCDO?

One morning, Francyn saw me dressed in an athletic shirt, putting on my running shoes.

"Where are you going? Are you going jogging?" she asked.

"Yeah."

"Can I come too?"

"OK, sure."

She ran off to put on her jogging pants and came back five minutes later with Khurt, Carlito, and their cousin Gelo who also lived in the compound. They clamored outside, excited to go "jogging." We decided to jog all the way to a park I hadn't visited yet called Camp John Hay. I had been told it was a beautiful park filled with lots of trees and picnic tables.

I set off at a brisk pace, naively expecting to get exercise from our outing. Francyn kept up for a while. Khurt and Carlito maintained a stop-and-go speed. Gelo lagged behind.

"He needs exercise," Gelo's mom told me before we left the house. "That's why I'm making him go with you."

"OK guys, let's go faster," I tried to encourage them as we reached a giant hill. Basically all of Baguio sat on a hill. If you weren't going down a hill, you were going up one. The entire city was nestled on an assortment of mountains, valleys, and everything in between. I stood behind Gelo and pushed him all the way to the top of the crest. Gasping and panting, he slowed down in hopes of stopping, but all the other kids were already far ahead so I just kept pushing him from behind.

Despite several rest breaks along the way, we finally made it to Camp John Hay. At the entrance, everyone had to stop first at the 7-Eleven store for a snack. Francyn had been put in charge of her younger brothers' money, so she dictated what they could and couldn't buy. Carlito accepted anything sweet and tasty, but Khurt didn't like his loss of choice.

"I want Coke!" he cried.

"You can't have it. Mama said no soda."

"Wahhh! I want it."

"No!"

His cries escalated into a tantrum, and we had no choice but to leave without buying him anything. I walked outside while drinking my iced tea and gave Khurt a sip so that he'd stop crying. He took a drink, and then another. He gulped it down.

"Hey! That's mine," I said as I tried to grab my drink back.

"No."

Exhausted from our "run" and with all the kids' energy depleted, we had to head home before entering the park. *Maybe next time I'll get to see the nice trees and grass.*

Weekend park outings became a regular activity. Occasionally, Gelo's mom or Francyn, Khurt, and Carlito's mom would come along as well. One morning we took a jeepney to Burnham Park in the city center. It was seven o'clock when we arrived, and already the park flourished with the activity of family picnics, loitering couples, or individuals bent on getting exercise in the crisp, fresh air. Exercise enthusiasts were everywhere—runners, joggers, walkers, bikers, and a few boaters on the touristy man-made lake. Groups of people practiced tai chi or martial arts, and there was even an aerobics class. Everywhere people milled about enjoying the early morning sunshine.

The aerobics instructor was an older Filipino man with an oversized shiny belly protruding out of his unbuttoned shirt, fat jiggling with each new dance move. His portable boom box blasted a combination of 70s and 80s hits remixed with dance beats. I couldn't decide if it was more entertaining to watch him or the people attempting to follow along to his peppy routine.

I jogged with my host family around the lake for a few rounds and then sat down on a bench to rest.

"So, Jollibee or McDo?"

"What?"

"Jollibee or McDo?"

I had been invited to breakfast at two of the most popular and frequented fast-food chains in the Philippines. McDo was just short for McDonald's, but Jollibee was a Filipino establishment. I was never one for eating much at fast-food restaurants, even in the US, and the prospect of eating greasy food for breakfast that morning seemed less than appealing. My body convulsed inside, pleading with me that such food would be a regrettable idea after such productive exercise in the park. But with the question still lingering and all eyes on me, all I could do was stammer. "Oh...um...hmmm."

What should one do in such a situation?

A. Choose Jollibee and suffer the consequences.
B. Choose McDo and suffer the consequences.
C. Suggest KFC just to see how they react.
D. Mutter something incomprehensible in the hopes they might forget about the whole idea.

Suffice it to say, option "D" didn't work. Someone chose Jollibee for me, and so we walked inside, past the shiny red plastic chairs, past the play place swarming with screaming kids throwing red plastic toy balls, and settled ourselves at a red plastic table. Gelo's mom asked what my order would be, and suddenly I felt caught off guard.

Again, what to do? Should I:

A. Order fries like Francyn.

B. Order Filipino spaghetti with hot dog chunks like Khurt and Carlito.

C. Order soda with ice cream like Gelo.

D. Convince my host family that I just want coffee for breakfast.

I told my stomach it would laugh about this one day.

One Saturday morning, Mama Ginny took me to the souvenir and handicraft section of the market. Francyn, Khurt, and Carlito, my usual companions, tagged along for fun. After being warned by numerous people about keeping a close watch on my belongings, I clutched my purse against my side. We wandered through the warm maze of stalls, merchants calling out, "Yes, ma'am sir, sir ma'am. Buy something."

Flustered by the amount of attention I was bombarded with from each new merchant, I avoided eye contact, pretending I wasn't interested in any products. But I did find it amusing that they always named whatever product I so much as glanced at, as if I had no clue what it was.

"T-shirt, ma'am."

"Slippers."

"Bags."

"Umbrella."

"Scarf, ma'am. Hats. Coin purse, ma'am."

The onslaught of nonstop calls for blankets, purses, and T-shirts continued aisle after aisle. I couldn't decide whether to laugh or be annoyed at their business tactics.

Mama Ginny decided she needed a manicure and told us to explore the other side of the market while we waited for her. In its entirety, the Baguio market covered several kilometers of land—row after row of stalls stacked to the ceiling with every type of goods imaginable. I loved the eclectic assortment of items for sale. Everything from plastic washing buckets, rain boots, and fresh produce to underwear, teacups, tobacco, and leggings. It took me several months to learn how to navigate my way around the entire market. Even then, I still managed to find new pockets of stalls that I'd never come across before.

As we walked past the fresh seafood stalls, we saw frogs jump from shallow buckets of water, and crabs clambered over one another trying to escape their containers. A live catfish gave a spastic flip of its tail, sending fishy water in its wake. Further along we found the meat section lit with the orange-reddish glow of dim bulbs, which revealed freshly butchered carcasses. Lazy circular fans spun just fast enough to ward off flies waiting to pounce on the trays of moist animal parts. Where no fans were to be found, vendors gave occasional flicks with towels or palm fronds.

I swatted some bumbling flies away from my face and I found myself staring straight into the eyes of a pig's head sitting on top of a butcher's block. I could just imagine it sitting in some family's kitchen, an old lola hacking away at it in preparation for some soup dish. She'd probably tell you that the ears were what made the soup taste delicious.

After an hour of aimless wandering, both of the younger ones were waning fast. Khurt downright refused to walk any farther, despite being the older of the two boys. I scooped him up and carried him for a while. His body grew heavy and limp like a laden sack of Baguio beans as he drifted off to sleep. But his warm head rested so snug against my shoulder that I had no complaints. That is until my limbs began to ache from the strain. I was unable to carry him any longer, so we returned back to where we had left Mama Ginny, who was just finishing with her pedicure and market errands. I walked with everyone back to the jeepney stop but didn't get on because I intended to meet up with another volunteer downtown.

"Why aren't you coming with us?" Khurt asked, now awake from his nap.

"I'm coming later. I'm just meeting my friend," I reassured him.

"Oh…OK." And then he added as an urgent afterthought, "I love you!"

"I love you too!" I couldn't help but smile. I waved goodbye, and he disappeared inside the jeepney.

## 9

## FOGGY WEATHER, FOUL MOOD

The weather in Baguio seemed to change as drastically as my mood. Mornings were bright and sunny, but by midday the fog rolled in, enveloping everything in a cloud so thick that I'd have to strain my eyes to see outdoors. One moment I could see houses of cement, rusty metal, and multicolored roofs covering the hillside slopes. The next minute, complete whiteness. It was so dense that it would drift into the room through an open window, its tendrils trailing mysteriously downward, thick and curling like a fog machine. It was as if I'd been immersed in the middle of a junior high Halloween dance.

"Wow, look at the fog!" I told my co-worker, Carmelita.

"Mmm-hmm," she responded, unperturbed.

"It's so thick!"

"Mmm-hmm."

It took a while before I got used to living inside a cloud. No big deal. It happened daily. But in those first few months, I was mesmerized by its reappearance day after day.

When I wasn't staring at the fog, I might be found staring at my computer screen, trying in vain to plan projects for no one in particular, just to keep myself busy. I volunteered myself to help other co-workers with random projects: leading games for a school celebration day, substituting for English grammar classes (not my favorite), and helping Carmelita with her theater group's upcoming performance. But after a few weeks, I still had nothing of substance or permanency that I could attach myself to. I had been working at my site for over three months, and I felt useless. No one seemed to understand why I volunteered there or what they wanted me to do. Perhaps they weren't sure what to make of me. They must have been asking themselves, "What should we do with this foreigner?" My growing boredom was coupled with growing frustration. *Why am I here? Am I even needed? What was the plan supposed to be again?*

The Peace Corps staff warned us of the first six months' slow period. It was the time for building strong relationships, they said. When the relationships were well established, then it would become easier to accomplish something, a project perhaps. Things took time. I claimed to be a patient person before moving to the Philippines, but then I learned that my patience was not nearly as adept as I needed it to be. *Things will happen in time.* I tried to console myself, without much luck.

~~~

My days at work were structured around the meal schedules of morning merienda, lunch, and afternoon merienda.

"Let's eat now!" co-workers would call out as they pushed me toward the lunchroom canteen. I ate lunch at my center every day, taking whatever option the canteen lady served. Typically she'd fill a partitioned plastic green plate with the *ulam* (main dish), a giant scoop of rice, and a bowl of broth.

"Yum! Thank you, Ate!" I called over the counter to the cook.

"You're welcome, ma'am," she blushed.

A lot of Filipino dishes consisted of comfort-food type stews and soups, and the canteen served many of them including *adobo,* one of the most well-known Filipino dishes. It consists of small chunks of meat and potatoes simmered in garlic, soy sauce, and vinegar. *Afritada* was another popular dish they served and is a stew made with meat, potatoes, carrots, and bell peppers cooked in tomato sauce. Some of the soups that I grew to love were *sinigang,* a sour soup made from tamarind fruit, and *tinola,* a savory chicken ginger soup with vegetable pieces called *sayote.* Sometimes the canteen would serve delicious specialties like Filipino barbecue, one of my favorites, or *tortang talong,* which was roasted eggplant soaked in egg and fried into a patty.

At first I would always ask the name of all the dishes served each day, suspicious of what I'd be eating. But after a while, I stopped asking and just ate it. Sometimes I had no idea what I was eating; I learned to just eat. I got used to most dishes and even craved them. My body started feeling hungry if I ate a meal absent of rice. I'd look forward to the hot savory bowl of broth with every meal. I loved eating bananas as a dessert like my co-workers often did.

But sometimes there were days when the only options were the inevitable fat dishes. I dreaded those days. Filipinos consider the large chunks of fat delicious, even better than a thick and tender piece of meat. Sometimes after pushing the squishy white cubes around my plate and filling up mostly on rice and a few bites of vegetables, I'd slip my plate back on the dish return table when no one was looking. But I was always fearful of giving the impression that I was wasting food.

I spent months forcing undesirable foods down my throat while my co-workers looked on with eager faces to make sure that I had enjoyed my meal.

"Do you like it, Teacher?"

"Oh, mmm, *masarap*! Tasty!"

"You eat more, hah!"

My stomach whined and cursed me. I told it to take one for the team on behalf of cultural understanding and integration. But when the initial attention of being a new volunteer wore off and I was left to my own devices at lunchtime, I avoided the things I disliked or disposed of them quietly. I might sweet-talk the lunch ladies into serving me something different or hide it under bowls of soup. In moments of crisis, I even resorted to pawning the unappetizing food off on the center's dog if he happened to be around. "Isang! Isang! Come here, boy! That's a good boy. That's right. Eat it up."

After lunch I would linger with some of the parents in the canteen and sip on coffee. I had at that point already become addicted to 3-in-1 coffee despite my self-protestations and declarations against such a deplorable product, an obvious insult to coffee. The Filipino style coffee, 3-in-1, is a sachet pouch of instant coffee, creamer, and sugar. Actually, it's mostly creamer and sugar. Maybe mostly sugar. I had finally given in to the sugar masquerading as coffee, and I now enjoyed it too. And coffee was always paired with *chika-chika*, gossip—both a regular part of merienda time.

Each day, my co-workers would take a break from working and hang about the office chatting away over their chika-chika, telling stories, and practicing English with me.

"Ate Debs, let's have merienda," they urged as they took out packets of chips or cookies.

"Hullo, hullo!" my supervisor would call out whenever he entered the office during merienda time. "It's time to have some 'vitamins,'" he'd exclaim with a wink and a jolly chuckle. "It's good for you!" Vitamins being the code word for unhealthy but accessible junk food. As a foreigner, it was important that I participate in merienda time. I learned to force myself to stop what I was doing and eat whatever it was that a co-worker had offered, anything from coconut-flavored munchies to frosting-coated crackers.

"Mmm! Sweet cheese crackers! Delicious!" Smack-smack. Smile.

Fortunately, I figured out that when I was handed several items at once, I could casually and discreetly stuff some of those snack packs in my desk, saving them for later when I could pass them off to kids who came to visit me during class breaks.

After several weeks of meriendas filled with unfamiliar snack foods, I longed for something that tasted like America. I begged family and friends to send me care packages filled with American goodies. Each time they arrived, I'd pile the Goldfish Crackers, Snickers, licorice, cookies, and cereal boxes on top of my bed. I would then proceed to devour the food with an unrelenting appetite, tearing at the packages with wild man-beast maneuvers. There was an unwritten rule amongst Peace Corps volunteers that if a care package was opened in the presence of other volunteers, the spoils had to be shared. That was why, more often than not, volunteers would proudly show off their brown boxes from abroad, but took care never to open them in public. That was a private affair for personal indulgence.

Volunteers also commonly used the term "Peace Corps goggles" to tease each other. It meant that the volunteer experience tended to skew one's perception of reality, and those who were out of touch with reality might be accused of wearing Peace Corps goggles. Using superlatives was a dead giveaway that one was wearing Peace Corps goggles. For example, I once ate an American-style pizza with real cheese and was so enamored by it that I consumed six large slices. I found it so delicious that I declared it was the *best* pizza I had *ever* had in my *life*! It wasn't. But I had been in a foreign country for several months without having eaten one ounce of real mozzarella cheese. At that point, anything semi-American tasting was the *best* thing I had *ever* eaten.

~~~

"Let's go, Ate Debs," Jocelyn said as she gathered up art supplies and game props. Twice a week I partnered with Jocelyn to lead an after-school program at three local public high schools. We were supposed to teach life skills, things like leadership, communication, responsibility, and other youth development activities. My favorite was when we played team building games. I gained some sort of satisfaction watching the teens squirm with frustration as they tried to complete a specific mission with their differently abled teammates. Depending on whether they decided to work together or not, the group dynamics escalated to either massive irritation in the face of failure or elation and triumph at the success of their completed task.

For this particular session, we had planned an almost impossible game that required teams to scoop up tiny beads from inside a circle drawn on the floor and pour them into their team's cup just outside the circle. The only materials allowed were long sticks fastened with a spoon at the end. The trick to the game was that if they tried to scoop up the beads with their own stick, it was impossible to put them in their own cup because the pole was much too long. However, it was very easy to drop the beads into the other team's cup. It was only toward the end of the session that one girl finally discovered that technique. Since most groups were already experiencing extreme frustration at their lack of success, anyone's success was more exciting at that point. They began collecting beads, and everyone cheered each time a new deposit dropped into a cup.

During the session, I noticed that more students kept drifting in through the door. Some I recognized as regulars, we usually had about eight of those. Others were students I had never met before. Jocelyn and I exchanged glances each time a new group of teens came inside. I could see in her eyes how shocked she was. Perhaps we were lucky that day. Perhaps our regulars had invited their friends. Whatever brought them there that day, it created new energy and enthusiasm in the room. Despite the difficulty of the bead activity, the students still watched each person's attempt with anticipation, slapped each other on the back, and made loud exclamations of "*Hay naku!*" which is the Filipino expression indicating a sigh of annoyance, fear, or relief.

After the session, Jocelyn and I headed to catch a jeepney back to the office. I turned to her, gave her a high five, and exclaimed, "Way to go, partner in crime!"

"We had twenty kids today, Ate!" she replied, still in awe about our session. A moment later, "Are you in a hurry, Ate? Do you want to get some barbecue?"

We had never done anything together outside of work, so I nodded yes. The sun drifted lower in the sky with soft orange and pink hues. We stood in the street watching the last rays disappear, waiting for the street vendor to grill some Filipino-style barbecue skewers for us. Jocelyn gave the man a few coins then took two finished skewers off the grill. She handed me one—intestines on a stick—and started munching on the other. A large Coke delivery truck stood parked at the far end of the street. "*Ito ay Happiness.* This is Happiness," the advertisement read, depicting a young man drinking a refreshing bottle of Coke. The ad had it all wrong, I thought to myself. It wasn't a bottle of coke but this—the triumph of moments like today—that brought happiness. *I may not be doing anything spectacular, but at least it was a step somewhere.* Even the smallest of triumphs needed celebration. To me, the little things brought the most joy, and if you looked hard enough, life in the Philippines was made up of lots of those little things.

## 10

# IT'S BEGINNING TO LOOK A LOT LIKE CHRISTMAS

I knew that the Christmas season had started in the Philippines once I began to hear Christmas songs being played at malls, restaurants, and cafés. That happened at the end of August. By September, even more songs could be heard, along with garlands, lights, colorful decorations, and *parols*, which are Philippine Christmas star lanterns. November was when the most impressive displays would be set up. Gigantic manger scenes outside churches, schools, and even McDonald's. Enormous Christmas trees were exhibited with pride in the city center, inside the SM Malls, and in the parks. Parols were everywhere. Some were flashy and tacky. Others were more intricate with a miniature manger scene crafted inside the center of the star.

That December, I went with my host family to a Christmas village—a life-sized, intricately decorated winter wonderland. I sat in the back of the taxi with Francyn, Carlito, Khurt, and Gelo, while Gelo's mom and Gelo's cousin, Jun Jun, sat up in the front. I recognized Jun Jun as one of the students at the school where I worked, and I heard him singing along to "Eye of the Tiger" playing on the radio. Only he mistakenly sang "eye of the fire" until Gelo teased him about it.

At the Christmas village, gingerbread houses, puffy snowmen, gaudy Christmas trees, and festooned lanterns made me feel like I was walking through an enchanting Christmas movie set. The most exciting part of the village was the "snow." As I looked up at the black starlit sky, dainty flakes fell on my face, scarf, and boots. A nearby sign read "Daily Snowfall Schedule." There were four times a day in which the snow machine sent fluffy bubbles into the air and made people dance for joy, dreaming of what snow was really like. Gelo, Jun Jun, and I extended our arms to the sky catching the "snow" on our jackets and faces. In some strange way, it felt magical to me. The small, white specks floated down against the dark night, and I started to miss the cold winters back home.

In the Philippines, one of the common Christmas traditions is called *Simbang Gabi*, a special novena in which Catholics attend mass every morning for the nine days before Christmas. Traditionally, the Simbang Gabi Mass is celebrated at dawn, sometimes as early as five o'clock in the morning. I decided that experiencing Simbang Gabi would be a fun way to get into the season, and so on the first morning of the novena, I forced myself to leave my cozy blankets before the sun had risen. When I left the house, the stars and moon were my only sources of light. *Who even gets up this early?* I complained to myself as I searched for a taxi in the dark. Apparently everyone and their brother, as I soon found out. Inside the cathedral, I squeezed into the half a seat I'd managed to find. Many unlucky parishioners were forced to stand at the back and sides for the remainder of Mass. *They do this for nine days?!* That was dedication indeed.

After the Simbang Gabi Mass ended, I bought some *bibingka* from a woman standing near the cathedral steps. Bibingka are rice cakes cooked in banana leaves. They're warm and sticky and resemble a thick puffy pancake. The morning light displayed pink streaks in the sky, and I could hear hints of a city just beginning to wake up. Taxi cabs raced by. Jeepneys snorted exhaust. Children chatted, arm in arm with comrades on their way to school. The clanging da-dang, da-dang of the garbage truck bell could be heard in the distance.

On Christmas Eve, I took Francyn and Gelo to the evening Mass at the cathedral. Like Simbang Gabi, people packed into the church more tightly than in the jeepney I rode for morning rush-hour commutes. We squeezed into the crowd, making our way up to the balcony, claiming a small corner space where we could stand. The heat from so many bodies rose to the ceiling, a suffocating, overbearing humidity that forced us to peel off our layers of scarves, jackets, and hats. So much for pretending it was a cold Christmas.

The choir sang pleasant harmonies, which echoed off the carved stone columns and filled the humid, sticky air like a delicious floral scent. During the song called "The Gloria," several parishioners maneuvered a giant-sized parol star along a rope pulley across the length of the church.

"Glory to God in the highest…" the choir sang out. Now lit and flashing red, gold, and green colored bulbs, the enormous star made its way, dangling across the congregation and reached the front of the altar where it hung for the remainder of Mass. My mouth opened wide, dumbfounded at first, and then I laughed. I could just imagine traditional American Catholics falling out of their seats at the impropriety of such a sacred moment. On occasion, when I told stories about my experience of Christmas in the Philippines, I got comments about it.

"That kind of display doesn't belong in Mass," they'd say.

"Just wait until you see what they do at Easter," I'd counter with a smirk. Christmas decorations with flashing lights were tacky to be sure, but somehow it fit the celebratory and joyous environment that I had become accustomed to living in. It fit the Philippines.

By the time Francyn, Gelo, and I arrived back home it was close to midnight. Most families celebrated *Noche Buena*, a tradition of waiting until after midnight to have a huge feast with abundant food, music, gaiety, and plenty of Red Horse Extra Strong beer or Emperador Light Brandy. I wandered between the houses in my host family's compound offering to help prepare or cook various dishes. At one o'clock in the morning, my stomach sent me painful, cramping hints that I needed food. *I thought we were just waiting until midnight?* That, of course, was simply normal Filipino time. It was ready when it was ready.

"Let's eat!" Mama Ginny called from the kitchen.

*Finally!* My stomach rejoiced. We gathered around the table, and with greetings of "*Maligayang Pasko!* Merry Christmas!" to one another, we consumed copious amounts of food. Then we went back and filled our plates again. My stomach began to burst over the lip of my jeans, and I contemplated changing into something more comfortable, like sweatpants.

Mama Ginny looked over at me and urged, "There's still more food! Get some more!" I surveyed the table filled with *lechon* (spit-roasted pig), *inasal* (skewered chicken), rice, pancit noodles, adobo, lumpia, and other things I couldn't name. I opted for one more serving of mango float, a dessert made with layers of graham cracker crumbs, thick cream, and fresh sliced mangoes. I couldn't resist. Then I changed into sweatpants. *I love Filipino party food!* The clock read three o'clock in the morning as I lay in a food coma on the couch, watching a movie with eyes half closed.

More fiesta food awaited me the following day. I had been invited by Gelo and his mom to a picnic at Camp John Hay with Jun Jun's family. Jun Jun and his two siblings also went to the school where I worked, and I recognized his mom, Ma'am Anna, as one of the parents I had coffee with during afternoon merienda time. At the picnic table, I tried to do my duty as an honored guest and eat as much as possible.

"Teacher, there's more food. Go and get!"

"OK, I'll take a break first."

"Don't forget to eat, Teacher!"

The park was a haven for those seeking warm sunshine and fresh air. Afternoon light streamed through the scented pine trees. It was hard to imagine that it was Christmas day given all the bright sunlight and warm weather; this was no chilly, wet Christmas like I was accustomed to in America.

~~~

"What's dis?" Khurt asked a few days later as he unearthed a package of cookies from my suitcase.

"Hey! That's mine!" I snatched them out of his hand, making a mental note to hide them somewhere different after he left the room.

Both of the younger boys, Khurt and Carlito, had become very close with me, sometimes a little too close. I'd be in my room relaxing after a long day at work when they'd come bursting in without knocking, then proceed to entertain me with stories of ninjas and vampires, look in my desk drawers, or go through my closet for toys or candy they suspected I was hiding.

"What's dis?" asked Carlito as he pulled out a headlamp. Then he discovered the headlamp's two lighting options— bright light and red light.

"It's like a ninja robot!" Khurt said as he first eyed the flashlight, and then swiftly grabbed it out of Carlito's hands. After that I heard a steady mix of pretend laser gun sounds from Khurt and crying from Carlito whose toy had been taken away.

"OK, that's enough of my light." I took it away and sent them upstairs to play.

But they wouldn't be gone for long. A closed door meant nothing to them. I guess I could have figured that one out by my first encounter with Khurt in the CR.

By the end of January, I had been living at my host family's house in Baguio for over three months—the minimum requirement to help new volunteers assimilate into their community. After that, a volunteer could choose to remain in their host family's house or find a place of their own to rent. While I loved spending time with my host family and felt like they had become a second family to me, I knew I needed more independence. I wanted to shop for my own groceries at the market, to cook my own food, and push myself outside of my comfort zone to explore and meet new people. My co-worker Jocelyn helped me find an apartment close to where we worked and I made preparations to leave my host family's house.

The day I moved out was difficult for Khurt and Carlito because they were a little too young to understand.

"Why are you leaving?" Khurt asked.

"I'm moving to a new house."

"But you don't like to live with us anymore?"

"No, I like living here! I'm just moving to a house that's closer to my work. Don't worry, I'll be back to visit."

"You're family now," Mama Ginny told me. "Your room is always available whenever you want to come stay." My temporary room had become "Ate Debbie's room." Even after I'd moved out and other volunteers stayed there, the two boys still called it my room. "Why are you in Ate Debbie's room?" they'd ask the newcomers.

## 11

## KNOCK-KNOCK

I moved to a little cement block house just outside the city limits where the air smelled slightly fresher and the streets were somewhat less claustrophobic. The one-hour commute on a crowded jeepney was no longer part of my day. Now I lived only a five-minute walk to my workplace, albeit uphill. As a result, I developed really good glute muscles.

My residence was precariously glued to the side of a mountain, and I enjoyed sitting on my veranda or on top of the cement roof where I hung my laundry and gazing far down into the valley.

"Just as long as there are no landslides, you should be safe," I was told by neighbors. The view across the valley overlooked enormous mountains upon mountains fading into the distance, sometimes even with a glimpse of the ocean beyond. Clouds drifted through in thick, puffy formations, giving me the feeling of living above the world. Like an island in the sky, surrounded by a sea of clouds.

Different types of days brought changing color schemes painted across the sky. During twilight, the black silhouetted mountains contrasted with crimson and cabernet sunsets melting into a blood orange sky. On rain soaked days, if the weather relaxed and the downpour exhausted itself, the sun would lower beyond the mountains leaving behind a radiant glow the color of ripe, lush mangoes, its rays stretching up to a cold pink and blue skyline further up into the atmosphere.

Every morning I woke up to an orchestra of crowing roosters, howling dogs, squealing pigs, talking neighbors, and kids playing in the streets. After my usual routine of a bucket bath, coffee, and spraying the occasional cockroach, I headed out for work. The children waved to me every time I walked down the street, enthusiastically shouting my name.

"Hello, Ate Debs!"

"Hi, Ate Debs."

"Who's that?" a little one would whisper.

"That's Ate Debs," another would reply knowingly.

"Oh. Hello, Ate Debs!"

Returning home from work resulted in more greetings from kids and curious stares from bystanders at the little store outside my house.

"You are American?" a skinny boy asked me one evening. He had been sitting on a cement curb a few feet from my door, and he tugged at his dusty orange shirt, stretching it unconsciously while he spoke.

"Yes, I just moved here."

"But you're Pilipino?"

"*Oo*, Yes."

"Oh! So you know how to speak Tagalog?"

"A little. What's your name?"

"Jayden."

I went over to join him when suddenly a cluster of curious children crowded my breathing space, eagerly asking questions. Where was I from? Why was I there? When was my birthday? Did I have a boyfriend? Jayden sat calmly, right by my side, looking up with his gentle eyes. He ignored the little kids' questions and continued talking with me.

"You play guitar? Can you teach me?" he asked.

"Of course!"

"When will we have lessons?"

"How about this Saturday morning?"

"OK. What time?"

"Maybe nine or ten?"

"Why not at six?"

"Six?! What time do you get up?"

"Sometimes five."

"Hmm, how about eight?"

"OK!"

After that first conversation, our friendship was solidified. He became a constant and loyal greeter each day when I came home from work.

The second day he jumped off the cement curb and ran toward me. "Hi, Ate Debs!" he hollered as he waved me down.

"Hello, Jayden!"

"Do you remember?"

"Remember what?"

"About guitar lessons."

"Yes, of course."

"OK. Eight, right?"

Some days he'd knock at random times, and when I answered the door, he'd just stand there bashfully trying to come up with an excuse for why he was there. One evening I arrived home later than usual. The fluorescent orange lamp shone over an empty street; all the kids had already gone home for the night. Suddenly, I heard the sound of running footsteps and then a pounding on my door. I opened it, and there stood Jayden, out of breath, shivering in the cool evening air.

"I brought back your UNO cards," he panted, handing me the deck. Then he just stood there still shivering despite his worn, oversized red sweatshirt.

"Umm…" Jayden ventured.

"Yes?"

"Can I borrow your Old Maid cards?"

"Of course."

My co-workers often asked me if I felt lonely living in a house by myself. Family structure and networks were a huge part of the culture, and to leave the support and protection of family was considered to be more of a foreign cultural idea.

"Where do you live?" they asked me.

"In Irisan."

"Who's your companion?"

"Just me. I live by myself."

"What?! Why?! Don't you get lonely?"

I often replied in the negative. The fact was that despite how much I tried, for the first few weeks living in my new house, I was never left alone for long. Every day there were always curious kids knocking on my door.

"Ate Debs, can we borrow the UNO cards?"

"Ate Debs, can we play guitar?"

"Ate Debs, will you come play with us?"

My house became party central every night of the week. After all, when you're ballin' in the UNO cards, everyone comes over. They'd leave their thin, frayed flip-flops in a messy pile outside my door and play games on my living room floor until I kicked them out.

Jayden wasn't the only one who was interested in learning guitar. There was a small, skinny girl named Chesa who lived one street up with her older sister and grandmother while their mother worked abroad in Canada. One day, Chesa came over with Jayden and asked if I could teach her guitar as well. And then she started coming over every day, just like Jayden. Sometimes she came over even *more* than Jayden did. Just like the roosters, I often groaned when I heard Chesa early in the morning.

Knock-knock.

"Ate Debs!" Chesa called out.

"Mmmm."

"Ate Debs?"

"Hmmm."

"Ate Debs, where are you?" Chesa murmured outside my door.

I opened my eyes and debated if I should get out of bed. I opened the window instead.

"Later," I mumbled as I poked my head out the window.

"Aww, why not now?"

"I'm not awake yet."

It wasn't long before life in the neighborhood soon developed into a predictable and yet comforting routine that involved a lot of knocking at my door.

Knock-knock.

"Yes, Jayden?"

"Ate Debs, can I play with your UNO cards?"

"OK, here." I handed him the now worn and tattered deck.

Jayden remained standing on my doorstep, stretching out his shirt absentmindedly with his hands.

"What else?"

"Ate Debs, can I play guitar?"

"OK, here." I handed him my guitar. He took it hesitantly, still lingering.

"Umm. Ate Debs?"

"Yes?"

"Can you teach me more songs?"

"Ohhh, OK, Jayden. Let's play some guitar."

Jayden, Chesa, her sister Charlene, along with Tala, Makayla, Angelica, Caleb, Jose, and Oreo were the usual crowd who frequented my doorstep. Oreo, a scruffy looking boy with a flop of disorderly hair, had such wide, round eyes that you could just see the mischief seeping out of them. He didn't say much, just hung around all the bigger kids and tried to do what they were doing. The kids called him *itlog*, which means "egg" in Tagalog. Maybe it was because he was so small. His real name, when shortened, sounded a lot like Oreo, so I asked if I could call him that. And then it stuck. All the kids started calling him Oreo. He had never eaten a real Oreo cookie before, so he didn't understand his nickname. That is, until I gave him some Oreos, and his eyes lit up. He liked his nickname after that.

I gave nicknames to a lot of the kids. There were so many of them that I could never remember their real names. It was easier to give them my own names, and they enjoyed that. Spiderman was one of those kids who loved it. One day when I came home from work, he was standing outside my house playing with a giant spider. When I made an I'm-really-scared-of-spiders noise, he found it funny and pretended to throw the spider at me, which caused me to jump and squeal. He just laughed.

"Ha, ha. Very funny, Spiderman." I put my hands on my hips and pretended to shake my head at him in disapproval. I still to this day cannot remember his actual name. The name Spiderman worked just as well, if not better. Every time I'd pass him in the street, he'd lunge at me and say "Spiderman" in a creepy zombie whisper.

"Oh hey, Spiderman," I'd respond with a smile.

In fact, that was probably the only thing he ever said to me.

"Spidermannnnn."

I got used to it.

One evening I heard the familiar knock-knock on my door. I opened it a few inches and saw Chesa standing outside.

"Will we have guitar lessons again?" she asked.

"OK, later. Maybe at eight tonight?" I was trying to hold my ground. A few weeks of curious and energetic neighbors and kids knocking on my door every single night had begun to get old. I needed space. I was tired of being the Americana who everyone watched and filled their chika-chika conversations with. I had planned on spending that evening listening to music, eating Oreos, and catching up on my writing. *I must be strong. I am in control. I am in charge of my own time.*

"How about seven?!" Chesa persisted. She was relentless, that one. I guess bargaining in this country didn't just apply to the market.

"Hmm, seven thirty then. I have some things to do first."

She peered into my house, wondering what I was doing. I tried to tell her I was writing, that I liked to write, that it was one of my hobbies. She still had a suspicious face but accepted my explanation and left.

Five minutes later I heard it again. Knock-knock. There were two of them now, Chesa and Jayden. "Why not now?" Chesa asked.

"OK, fine. Now. And then you go home for dinner afterward." So much for holding my ground. It was hard to say no when there were two cute kids standing on your doorstep.

**12**

## WHAT ARE YOU DOING, ATE?

It was during my sophomore year in high school that the movie *Josie and the Pussycats* came out. My friends and I watched it together, and like many other teen girls of our generation, we left that movie theater starry-eyed and inspired, knowing that it was our destiny to start a girl band. My friend said she'd learn bass, another would learn drums, one friend was already taking voice lessons, and I volunteered to learn guitar. We routinely got together at each other's houses, drank Mountain Dew, munched on chocolate and gummy worms, and wrote songs for our band.

As I taught myself how to play guitar, music became an essential part of my life. I clung to my guitar like a precious possession, gleaning support from it in difficult times and strumming out tunes of joy for the better days. I was never completely at ease unless I was holding a guitar in my hands. Thus, when I left for the Peace Corps, I was armed with one suitcase, one backpack, one carry-on, and the fourth and last piece of allowed luggage was my guitar. With that guitar I began to do useful things.

One afternoon, Carmelita approached me and asked if I would teach guitar lessons at the center where we worked.

*Finally! Something to do!* There were six boys from the fifth grade who were interested in learning. The Pinesview School Guitar Club was officially formed, and I began teaching my little pupils each day after school. Jun Jun, Samuel, Esteban, and Ma'am Ligaya's son, Benji, were regulars. Only Samuel had his own guitar—a black, scratched, warped, and rusted piece of work—so we shared my guitar and rotated it every few minutes so each person got a chance to practice.

"Like dis, Teacher?" they'd ask, looking for approval.

"Yes, correct, very good!"

Guitar Club became my new life, and I threw myself into chord charts, music booklets, and reassurances of "keep trying, you'll get there." I wasn't sure if that was what I was supposed to be doing—I didn't think I could save the world by teaching music after all—but I was tired of the inactivity and boredom while I waited for direction that never seemed to come. I needed an outlet for my passion. I needed to do something useful. Teaching music was something useful.

Things I've learned thus far in the Philippines:

1. UNO cards help you learn numbers, colors, *and* make friends.
2. Patience is a virtue. I have very little.
3. A guitar will help you do useful things.

My guitar was too bulky for the small frames of my fifth-grade students. As each took their turn in practicing new chords or melodies, their skinny arms hung in awkward contortions over the wooden body, stretching in earnest determination. Even though Samuel had his own guitar, he still liked to play on mine because his guitar sounded more like clashing metal than anything resembling an instrument. However, reaching the sound hole on my guitar became so cumbersome for him that he resorted to playing over the fretboard instead.

At first, I assumed Samuel was shy. He typically spoke to me only in short phrases or mumbled words. Every time he had to say something to me, his face would blush red despite his dark complexion, and he'd look away, trying not to laugh out of embarrassment. They called him Binay because his face had an uncanny resemblance to the vice president, Jejomar Binay. His face turned red at that too.

If I looked at his smile, I would see his *pasaway* side—always playing practical jokes and somehow getting away with mischievous deeds with one flash of a grin. But when I looked at his eyes, I saw something different. It was the "Samuel look." The first time I witnessed it was right before the Guitar Club's first performance.

"OK, guys. Make sure to smile when you're on stage," I directed my six little pupils. "Look at each other when you start, OK? Samuel and Jun Jun, you'll do the solo, yeah?" Jun Jun nodded as he gripped my guitar with white knuckles. Samuel stared at me, horrified.

"Don't be nervous, guys. You're going to do great!" I encouraged, and gave everyone a high five. Then, just before I walked over to the audience to take my seat, I caught Samuel's eye. In that one second, it was like I could see the thoughts running through his mind. A door had been opened for him, and he was invited to pass through it. It was as if I held the world in the palm of my hand, and I was giving it to him. I gave him a big, cheesy smile. He blushed then walked on stage.

It wasn't until months later that I connected Samuel to the woman with the crying baby. The boarding house Ma'am Ligaya had taken me to during a community visit—the place with the dark hallway and the room with one green square curtain—was Samuel's house. My mind was a swirl of conflicting views as I watched Samuel each day at school. Despite being similar in size to my guitar, he was intelligent, funny, and lived with a tenacity that helped him move through life where others might have given up. His nimble, slim fingers danced up and down the guitar fretboard with ease. He'd solo through several bars of chords before getting self-conscious and look up with a questioning glance, his eyes seeking feedback for whether or not he had done a good job. He smiled his mischievous smile, he laughed, he joked, he had a crowd of friends, and he got high grades. Samuel always appeared very happy, and not just superficially so, but genuinely filled with joy. That was the same for most kids I encountered during my time in the Philippines. They were joyful and energetic youth who had so much love to give despite whatever they went home to after the school rang its final dismissal bell.

~~~

By the next semester, I suddenly found myself not only the Guitar Club teacher but also the director of the brand new choir at my school. Standing up in front of a classroom of kids was not a big deal for me because I had worked with youth for most of my life. But standing up in front of a swarm of Filipino children, trying to command some sort of attention and authority while they giggled at my American accent and funny way of pronouncing "*umupo kayo*, sit down," gave me a sense of both excitement and dread.

The principal gave me a list of students who had signed up to be in my class. Twelve kids. Perfect. Enough to sing as a choir but small enough to manage. I could handle that.

The day of my first class came. The room echoed with the clamor of plastic desks being pushed or dragged across the cement floor. The helpful kids moved enthusiastically to clear a space. The unhelpful kids stood around and did nothing. I was using my best American accent to direct the arrangement of chairs for the choir when the principal walked in with a group of students.

"You have a few additional kids who signed up." She motioned them inside.

*Oh! Great!* I looked at the moving mass of pleated, olive green uniforms and counted. Thirty-one kids. *Wait, thirty-one?!*

My dreams of being the most amazing, savvy children's choir director disintegrated on that first day of class. The kid up front who insisted on shouting each song was the first indicator. Then there were the five boys in back who refused to listen, crawling and hiding under tables instead. Two girls giggled whenever I tried to lead a singing warm-up. Actually, everyone giggled whenever we sang warm-ups.

"I'm working with kids, not professional singers" was my daily mantra. Then, putting on a big smile and my best happy-teacher voice, I taught them "Do Re Mi" from *The Sound of Music*. Our keyboard couldn't play "middle C" and sometimes "F," so I opted for singing a cappella songs instead.

The following day, a polite and soft-spoken third grader came up to my desk in the office.

"Yes?"

"Teacher, will we have singing class again today?"

"Not until next week," I informed her.

The next day she approached me again. "Teacher, are you sure we don't have singing class today?" Her friend had accompanied her this time, just to check that there hadn't been any singing classes that they'd missed.

"Don't worry," I assured them, "you won't miss out."

The next week I made thirty-two copies of the song we were going to sing and handed them out. Some kids still didn't get a copy. *How did that work out?* I counted the mass of olive green uniforms once again. There were forty kids this time.

I'd never directed a real choir class before, but I threw myself into the fray, trying to figure out how to be that perfect choir director I aspired to be. One of the intriguing dilemmas of being a volunteer is that even if you knew nothing about what you were trying to accomplish, you were still considered the resident expert on that subject. I suspected that incorrect assumption derived from the fact that I was American. I had credibility I hadn't earned. Luckily, Google came in handy a lot.

Things I have googled in the Philippines:

      — How to hip hop dance
      — What is an adjective?
      — How to pronounce English words
      — Tips for new choir directors

## 13

## WHAT'S IT LIKE IN AMERICA?

I may have lived in a cement box stuck on the side of a mountain, but I had an amazing view. That might have been the only redeeming quality of that house. Nothing could beat that stretch of landscape with mountains upon mountains. I'd often lie in a hammock gazing through the rusted railing of my veranda, reveling in my "million-dollar view," as I liked to boast.

Sounds of everyday life drifted up from the valley below. Sometimes it would be church services, weddings, or videoke sessions. Often it was roosters, dog fights, jeepneys, motorbikes, construction, or children walking to school. But occasionally, pig squeals resounded all over the hillside. There's nothing like waking up to the sound of a pig being slaughtered far down in the valley. The piercing cries resembling a half screaming pterodactyl, half angry elephant seared straight into my brain. The echoes would reverberate even through cupped hands; covering my ears made no difference. *Hay naku!* The decibel of noise emitting from the lungs of those poor creatures meant only one thing. Someone was having a party in the neighborhood today.

I can remember the first time I watched a pig get slaughtered. An old lolo in the neighborhood had passed away, and the family held a traditional funeral celebration. For several days, the outside of my house never lacked a loitering crowd. Relatives and friends lounged in the sunlight, chatting, playing cards, drinking, and eating. Two rather large pigs were tethered to the pine tree next door. I eyed their hairy bodies with nervous anticipation.

It was the squealing that brought me to the door. I peered outside with caution. Six men attempted to hold the squirming pig in their grasp. I saw Jayden and his cousin sitting in the grass with the neighborhood boys, eyes locked on the action. The pig was a strong fighter, but the knife had already begun to do its work. I stood transfixed, watching the scene before me as the screams and squeals lessened. Then, not wishing to watch any longer, I retreated back into my house and shut the door.

Later that day, a fire was built in the same lot, and the prepared pig was hoisted on a stick to roast for the next few hours. By the time the meat was cooked and the huge vats of red mountain rice were ready for serving, my entire neighborhood had shown up, sitting in the grass, crowding around the *sari-sari* variety stores, and even sometimes standing right outside my door. Somehow enough plates and spoons were produced, and everyone had their fill.

The second pig, still tied to the tree, had no idea what was coming for him the next day.

~~~

"Was that a chicken outside your house?" my family and friends would often ask as they balked at the animal calls and grunts they heard in the background over glitchy Skype conversations.

"Did I just hear a pig?"

"Why are those goats so loud?"

"Welcome to my world," was all I'd offer in reply. Welcome to the Philippines, I'd think to myself with a half smirk and shrug of the shoulders. There was no other response, no satisfactory answer that could explain the world in which I found myself. My home life in America consisted of the familiar hum of the refrigerator, a crunch of my roommate's tires on the driveway, the neighbor's lawn mower in the distance, or sprinklers coming on in the early morning. In the Philippines, my life was characterized by the sounds of animal calls echoing from the valley, customers coming to and from my neighbor's store, and little kids knocking on my door. In order to understand the Philippines, you had to experience the sounds and movement of the neighborhood.

Even though the Philippines was inundated with American retail chains, imitated pop culture and fashion trends and carried multiple American products, the difference between the two cultures was still evident. America and the Philippines were worlds apart.

"So, you are American?" my neighbor, Ate Malaya, asked me one day.

"Yes."

"But you're Pilipino?" She scrutinized my facial features.

"Yes, my dad is Filipino."

"So, you're half-half?"

"I guess so."

Ate Malaya sat all day long in her eight-by-three foot sari-sari store, the one attached to the end of my house. Every night she and her husband would sleep there too. Sari-sari stores were small convenience stores, stocked with junk food, instant noodles, drinks, and common household items. They also became a major contributor to my laziness when it came to doing actual shopping.

"What is it like in America?" Ate Malaya liked to ask. "Do they also have sari-sari stores?"

"What is it like in America? Do they have stray dogs running around?"

"What is it like in America? Do they ride on jeepneys?"

"What is it like in America? Are Americans very rich?"

Ate Malaya wasn't great at English and I was horrible at Tagalog, so we made a good team. She taught me Tagalog words, and I taught her English words. Sometimes we'd sit in the evening outside her store, pouring through my English-Tagalog dictionary, looking up words for fun.

I never imagined I'd ever come to a point in my life where I would actually look up words in the dictionary for fun. Then again, I also never foresaw that UNO cards and a guitar would be my main tools for making friends. Or that most of my closest companions in the neighborhood would be a crew of energetic nine-year-olds and a sari-sari store owner. And yet, there I was.

## 14

## YOU HAVE A VERY BIG GUITAR

They were rambunctious. Too much energy held inside a kid will inevitably explode like confetti from a New Year's Eve popper. Guitar Club that particular day became the moment when the string was pulled. My six students and I sat in a circle. Today was soloing day. We were working on improvisation skills over a simple blues song I had taught them recently. Between Jun Jun's fidgeting and Esteban chasing the girls in the classroom there to clean the blackboard, I should have known what was coming. To the girls' dismay, Benji bounced up to write on the newly cleaned blackboard. Samuel tapped them from behind and then ran away. Esteban took a break from chasing girls to strum a few chords, and then Jun Jun grabbed the guitar to try out his solo. They were behaving like monkeys.

I tried to sustain some sort of order by providing structure. "OK, Esteban, first you solo, and then you stop," I instructed him.

"Then," pointing at Benji, "you solo, and then you stop."

"And then you solo," nodding to Samuel, "and then you stop."

"You solo, you stop! You solo, you stop!" chanted Samuel in a sing-song rhythm.

"You solo, you stop! You solo, you stop!" repeated Jun Jun.

"You solo, you stop! You solo, you stop!" the other boys joined in the chant.

"You solo, you stop! You solo, you stop! You solo, you stop! You solo, you stop!" they chanted in unison as they danced around the room. Jun Jun started beatboxing with his mouth, and the chant turned into a rap song, their heads bobbing to the beat. The blackboard girls giggled.

"Boom, takt, boom-boom, takt. You solo, you stop. You solo, you stop."

I just sat there in the circle of now empty chairs and laughed. Any attempt to teach that day resulted in another outburst of the "You Solo, You Stop" rap. I had to remind myself that not all days will be productive days and shook my head in defeat.

Whether or not they were productive, my boys showed up to every practice. Even when their strumming sounded more like clanking, I could sense improvement.

"Like dis, Teacher?" Esteban asked.

"Yes, very good!"

"How about me, Teacher?" Benji asked.

"Oh…umm…just keep practicing."

"Watch me, Teacher. I can play da blues scale," Samuel boasted. "Wait, I'll start again. One more time, Teacher. I almost did it. Keep watching!"

"Uh huh."

"Are you still watching? I'll do it again."

They were the original six students, but soon others began inquiring about more types of music classes. Apparently, there had been talk at my school about creating a music program in the past, but it hadn't materialized just yet. So one day I set about trying to put one into action. We already had guitar and singing covered. Jocelyn played piano and said she could teach classes, and my other co-worker, Jay Ar said he could teach some bass. Putting together the music program was sporadic at first. I tried all sorts of things to test out what would stick. As part of the new music program outreach, I started going once a week to the local Social Development Center (SDC), a home for boys in conflict with the law, and taught guitar lessons.

Just before one of my first sessions at the SDC, I slipped into my guitar case straps, adjusted the guitar on my back, and started the fifteen-minute walk to the center.

"Hello! Where are you going?" a man called from the doorway of his internet shop. It was more like a shack than a shop, to be honest.

"Just there. To the SDC."

"Why you going dere?"

"I'm teaching guitar."

"You hab a bery big guitar."

"Yep. Thanks."

"See you later!"

"OK, bye."

*Who was that?* I chuckled to myself. Sometimes when I had conversations with random strangers on the street, it made me smile. It was another reminder of how friendly Filipinos could be, even if it seemed strange at times.

The SDC boys were all in their teenage years with ugly tattoos, knockoff brand baseball caps, and baggy pants. They tried to act really tough around me.

"Hey! It's Ma'am Debs! Ma'am Debs is coming." The boys would shout from the top of the hill.

"Hello, Ma'am Debs!"

"HEY! Ma'am Debsssss!!!!!"

"MA'AM      DEBS!!!      HELLO      MAAAAMMM DEEEEBBBSSS!!!

I waved back from the bottom of the hill. I couldn't even see who was shouting at me yet. *How did they know it was me? Must have been the giant guitar on my back.*

"Hey! What's-her-name is here."

"She's Ma'am Debs, you idiot!"

"Ma'am Debs! HELLO! HELLO MA'AM DEBS!!!"

"MAAAAAAAAM DEEEEEEBBBBBSSS!"

I laughed as I waved back.

When I first started teaching at the SDC, in an attempt to demonstrate the importance of treating instruments with proper care and respect, I asked each boy what their most valuable possession was. One shared that his cell phone was the most important. Another couldn't decide, and a third one replied that it was his *tsinelas*, his flip-flops. I looked down at his tsinelas, the scrappiest worn pair of tsinelas I had ever seen. Either he misunderstood the question or that boy owned only one pair of tsinelas.

Guitar lessons at the SDC went well, but even more than guitar music, the boys were into rap. Another Peace Corps volunteer, Andrew, had been working at the SDC a year prior to me and had set up a space in the library where the boys could compose their own rap songs. Eventually we teamed up to do a rap music composition and recording workshop. I wasn't skilled in rapping or composing a rap. I even tried it with them once:

*My name is Ate Debs,*

*I'm a Peace Corps volunteer,*

*I play guitar and I like it here.*

"How about that? Was it cool? Do I sound like a real rapper?" They just looked at me with raised eyebrows. I decided rapping wasn't my true calling.

For the SDC boys, however, lyrical words poured from their mouths as soon as the beat shook the speakers. We simply taught them how to use recording software on our laptops and let them be in charge of how they would edit and produce their compositions.

A few weeks later when I arrived for another recording workshop, I was greeted at the entrance by two of the high school boys. Instead of the usual "HELLO MAAAAM DEEEBBSS!!!" greetings, they ran up to me with scribbled lyrics grasped in hand, rapping their songs to me like they were on the stage.

"Wow, looks like you guys have been busy."

Without a reply, their rapping continued to an imaginary audience, and I followed them to the library where Andrew was setting up speakers for the "recording studio." The library studio was a decent set-up; the only drawback was that when it rained, the noise through the open windows was so loud that it would ruin the recording quality of the boys' songs. They didn't appear to notice the difference though. They were just as eager to record their rap songs be it in a heavy downpour with noisy boys out in the hallway or in perfect silence.

~~~

"Hey Debs, this is Khyle. He's new," Andrew introduced me.

"Hi, Khyle. Do you like rapping?" I asked him.

"Yes, ma'am. I do."

We soon discovered that Khyle's talent dripped out of him like the overflowing plastic rain barrel outside the library. His musical ability was personal, innate, and reverberated from deep within his soul. His lips moved with a natural grace and ease. Anything he created had passion, honesty, and an ability to draw others right into his music. I noticed that the other SDC boys recognized it too. Khyle was *cool*. Khyle was a *real* rapper. They looked up to him with reverence.

During Khyle's first recording session, everyone sensed the energy he emitted. They knew that something different, something big was taking place in the room that day. It was like watching a suspenseful movie. The closer we got to finishing the song, the more immersed the boys became. They were mesmerized in anticipation, staring at the screen each time the red record button was pushed, watching in awe at what came out of Khyle's mouth as he effortlessly rapped to the beat or sang the chorus with raw passion. They leaned in closer. It was as if by being there and watching the process, you felt like you were part of something, like you had written and recorded the song yourself. The boys all slapped each other on the back when it was finished, congratulating one another, I guess, for being present and being part of the action.

The most common song lyric the SDC Boys used was *makinig ka*, which expressed "listen up!" They rapped like music was their only chance to say how they really felt, express how they'd been treated, how they'd lived, who they were now. They weren't afraid to rap about their personal lives: the drugs, the bad influences, the gang members. Some had evident, built-up anger, while others were so respectful and kind that I wondered what it was they had done to get themselves arrested.

One afternoon after an unproductive recording session, the boys settled for taking silly photos on my laptop instead. They giggled like little children as the camera angle smashed and contorted their faces in hilarious positions. Despite their dark sunglasses, intimidating tattoos, and large chain necklaces, I was pretty sure they were just young, energetic, and lovable boys.

## 15

## TAMBAY-TAMBAY

Clad in my faded Gonzaga University sweats and a baggy shirt I purchased at an *ukay-ukay* secondhand store, I grabbed a handful of pesos and headed outside. My hair was styled in that uncombed, tousled, just-out-of-bed look. Gentle light streamed down on the mountain ridges, highlighting the rugged peaks and hills. Dipping downward, the sunlight rippled across the valley toward me, illuminating the homes dotted along the sloping hillside.

People stared at me as I walked down the street. It wasn't because of what I was wearing; they wore their *pambahay* lounging clothes too. Staring was just a part of the culture.

"Good morning, madam!"

"Hello, Ate Debs."

"Hello, Ate Bevs."

"Ate Devs."

"Hullo, Ate Bebs!"

The growing deviations of my name made me smile broader today. It was a typical linguistic confusion with Filipinos that certain consonants were swapped or sounded the same. A common switch was "P" and "F." Filipino was pronounced Pilipino. "That's so funny" sounded more like "that's so punny." "D," "V," and "B" also sounded very similar, and thus my name roved the gamut of pronunciations from Debs, Devs, Bebs, Bevs, and the like. It happened more with the younger kids since they had trouble pronouncing everything in general, but adults were just as guilty. Even the electricity meter outside my house was labeled "Devora."

This morning, I was on a mission for coffee. I hadn't bought coffee at the market because I knew that I could just buy it at Ate Malaya's sari-sari store. Except, on that lovely Saturday morning, her window was boarded up. Closed.

My neighborhood wandering led me down to a hidden sari-sari near Jayden's house, run by his family. I gave the kuya six pesos for a 3-in-1 coffee sachet packet. Heading back to my house meant another round of staring.

"Hello, madam!"

"Hi, Ate Debs."

"Hello, Ate Bevs."

"Hello, Ate Devs."

"Where did you come from?"

"What did you buy?"

Everyone always wanted to know where I was going, where I had come from, and what I had bought. It was just another way of saying hello.

"Where are you going, Ate?" a girl called out to me as I passed her on the street.

"There at the store. And you?"

"Just buying something too."

Filipinos didn't actually care about the specifics of your business but felt it imperative to ask. It was about connection and relationship more than content. Meeting someone new for the first time meant I'd get the introductory questions, such as "How much is your rent?" or, "Are you married?" and a lot of times, "Do you have a boyfriend?" I observed that short or general replies were sufficient enough to satisfy the questioner.

"What are you doing, Ate Debs?"

"Nothing," I'd answer casually.

"Where are you going, Ate Debs?"

"Up," I'd answer as I pointed at the hill with my lips.

"Hi, Teacher! Where are you going?"

"There."

In fact, not asking a friend you met on the street where they were going, where they had come from, what they were doing, or whether they had eaten yet was considered rude. So I began embracing the curious and inquisitive nature of greetings and tried to brainstorm fun, creative answers. There were always plenty of opportunities to try out my new responses because there were always people standing along the street or congregating around the sari-sari stores.

"Good apternoon," a neighbor called out to me as I passed him and his group of *tambay* friends. The smell of beer and smoke drifted in my direction.

"Good afternoon," I returned.

"What is good in de apternoon? It's your pace looking at me. Ha, ha!"

Laughter ensued. I just smiled.

Tambay, which suspiciously sounds like standby, was a regular pastime. It consisted of hanging out at the sari-sari stores or street curbs, trading bits of news or neighborhood gossip, and usually smoking two-peso cigarettes and drinking liter bottles of Red Horse Extra Strong beer. And staring. Tambay always involved watching everyone and everything that was going on.

I used to wonder why Filipinos liked to stare. *What's with the tambay culture? Don't they have anything better to do than stand around and stare at other people walking by?* There wasn't a whole lot I could do except to just ignore it, until one day I decided that I would stare back. When the five guys sitting on top of a passing truck stared at me, I stared right back. They waved. I stared at the tambay men, and they smiled back at me. I stared at the taxi driver staring at me, and he gave me a toothless grin. I stared at everyone. And then suddenly staring didn't feel weird anymore. I'd just keep looking at them, and they in turn kept looking at me. I always wondered who those strangers were and what their story was.

Things I've learned thus far in the Philippines:

1. Staring is ok, once in a while.
2. "Just there" is a normal response.
3. Sari-sari stores make you lazy.

I was starting to get into the rhythm and routine of my neighborhood life. The sounds that came up from the valley became normal. I was used to the tambay men and their staring. The greetings or questions from neighbors continued. I admitted my dependence on sari-sari stores. And the knocking. The door knockers were a constant source of entertainment.

Knock-knock. I knew who it was.

Knock-knock. *Maybe if I stay quiet, she'll go away.*

Knock-knock. "Ate Debs!"

Sigh. I pulled myself off the bed and answered the door.

"Ate Debs, what are you doing? Why you don't answer?" Chesa demanded.

"Oh…umm…I just did."

"Can I borrow your guitar?"

"OK, fine," I grumbled. Chesa was ruthless in her insistence at showing up in my life. Sometimes the introverted side of me—the one that needed time to myself—resisted her. But most days, I welcomed her presence.

One evening, Tala and Charlene stopped by and declared, "Ate Debs, let's be a choir!" Out of the neighborhood girls who regularly came by my house, Tala, Angelica, and Chesa's sister, Charlene, were best friends. Occasionally they let Chesa tag along as the fourth wheel.

"Yes, let's be a choir," Angelica echoed. They knew I worked with the choir at my school, and while they belonged to a different elementary school, they wanted to be part of a choir too.

"OK," I agreed.

Chesa and Jayden's older brother, Ronald, acted as the guitar accompanists. Angelica, Tala, and Charlene became the choir. As they attempted to get through the song, everyone was off-key, off-tempo, and off-melody. No one seemed to notice but Chesa. She struggled to play a constant rhythm while at the same time match the unpredictable dynamics of the singers. They were very unpredictable, wavering between flat and sharp, and never on perfect pitch. Chesa screwed up her face and gave me a confused grimace. It made me laugh out loud. I restarted everyone, this time on the same tempo. We'd have to work on the vocals.

Chesa reminded me of myself and my own thirst for learning guitar. She exuded an independent spirit, spoke her mind, and wasn't afraid of the boys. And she didn't shy away from a challenge. Over the next few weeks, her guitar skills developed rapidly, and I began preparing new songs in anticipation of her arrival each day.

Knock-knock.

"Where have you been?" I asked. "I thought you were going to come earlier."

"My grandmother said I had to do chores first."

"OK, well here's a new song for you. Give it a try."

"OK, Ate Debs."

"Chesa, you'll come again tomorrow, no?"

"Yes, Ate Debs."

~~~

While weekend days were spent trying to fend off the regular door knockers, I spent the evenings practicing my tambay skills, sitting outside Ate Malaya's store engaged with the usual exciting activities.

"How do you say heart in Tagalog?" I asked Ate Malaya as I flipped randomly through my dictionary.

"*Puso.*"

"How do you say mountain in Tagalog?"

"*Bundok.*"

"Ate Malaya, are there any traditional sayings in Tagalog?"

"*Kung may tiyaga, may nilaga.* It means if you have perseverance you have nilaga."

"What is nilaga?"

"It means...ay...what is nilaga in English?" she asked David, another neighbor friend.

"It means like a meal on da table. If you have perseverance, you will be rewarded with good things," he explained. David and his two friends, Rafael and Tomas, had become my most recent companions. Our shared love of playing guitar had bonded us. We jammed on the cement ledge in front of Ate Malaya's store every evening. I had purchased a top-hits songbook at the bookstore, and that became almost as popular as the UNO cards. Ate Malaya taught me some of the Tagalog songs, and whenever we sang, the tambay men came over to join in our sing-along. Now, instead of just having neighborhood companions who were mostly under the age of ten, I had several adult friends too.

David and Tomas were about my age and both lived on the same street as me. Tomas was Jayden's older brother (there were a lot of kids in that family) and was sweet and friendly but shy, as many Filipinos were. David, on the other hand, spoke English with confidence and had no problem conversing with the new Americana in the neighborhood. He lived at the corner of our street where the jeepney dropped people off. Every time I went to catch a jeepney, David's mom would greet me or tell me how nice I was or give me random fruit from her backyard.

Even though I tried to converse with my neighbors in Tagalog, sometimes it was really nice to have someone speak to you in clear English like David did. Until I had lived abroad, I never realized just how comforting it was to hear your native language. During those days, I was constantly surrounded by people and yet still felt lonely. Just being able to converse with someone in English helped me to stay sane, like I had someone I could talk to who might understand me.

"I made another friend today!" I boasted to a volunteer via text. When living in a foreign country, making a friend felt like a huge accomplishment. It was such an achievement that I wished I could've included it in my next Volunteer Report.

> Item 1: Conducted three community workshops for forty people.
> Item 2: Hosted one music workshop for twenty-five children.
> Item 3: Made a real friend.

## 16

# WHERE DID YOU COME FROM, ATE?

Several months into my service, I took a short vacation to Iloilo City, the hometown of my dad, which was situated on the island of Panay. I felt the time had come to do a little investigating into my roots and learn more about where my dad grew up. He'd mentioned he still had some distant relatives in the area, and although he had never met them, he managed to find a contact number for me. I texted the number for a younger cousin of his named Theresa. "Hi, this is Deborah Francisco. My dad told me to contact you since I will be in Iloilo this weekend."

"Yes...So when u going 2 arrivd here in Iloilo and what time?"

"I arrive at 8pm."

"OK...we will be going 2 be there at arround 7pm in the airport...we will be having a banner named DEVERO FRANCISCO...we were excitd 2 see u..."

As I walked out of the tiny Iloilo airport, a wave of sticky tropical heat engulfed my body. I wasn't sure what my relatives looked like, but I scanned the crowd of sign-holding greeters. Sure enough, my eyes caught a large green sign scribbled with a marker that read: "DEVERA FRANCISCO." I waved and smiled at them. I noticed that they were all shorter than me. I'm only five feet four, but I felt tall next to them. Theresa greeted me with a hug and then introduced me to the rest of the family.

I had been looking forward to this trip not only because I would be able to explore my dad's hometown but it would also be my first solo trip. I'd been dreaming about the prospect of getting lost in the moment. I had this romanticized idea that I'd be able to go where I pleased, explore, get lost, take my time, and just soak up the culture. Clearly, I underestimated Filipino hospitality. After meeting my relatives at the airport, they insisted I sleep at their house that night since it was late already. I was given someone's bed in the only air-conditioned room in the house. I was grateful for that.

The next morning, I lounged at the table eating pancit noodles, eggs, rice, and pandesal bread while my relatives watched.

"You want sweet potatoes?"

"How about more pandesal?"

"Have some coffee."

"You eat more, hah."

"So, what are your plans today?" Theresa asked me.

"Well, I was planning on taking a jeepney to visit the historical churches," I explained.

"Oh, you don't ride the jeepney! We drive you." Everyone else nodded.

"Oh, I don't mean to trouble you…"

"No trouble. We'd like to come too!"

I had suddenly accumulated several new travel companions. Realizing that my initial plans of wandering aimlessly and exploring in solitude and reflection were now thrown out, I gathered my energy and prepared for whatever the day would bring me. It was out of my control, and I went forward with an inward sigh of *bahala na* and a smile. Bahala na is a common

Filipino expression that is used to show acceptance of a situation you cannot control and can be translated in several ways: it's up to God, it is what it is, or just go with it. Today I embraced it—bahala na. Besides, it dawned on me that expecting to tour my dad's hometown without my relatives seemed strange. After all, hadn't I come to learn more about my family's history?

Things I've learned thus far in the Philippines:

1. Patience. Patience is a virtue.
2. Flexibility is a requirement.
3. Bahala na!

"You like lunch? We go to dis nice place," Theresa told me as all the relatives packed into the car. I was already forgetting who was who.

We pulled into the SM Mega Mall parking lot. "We like going to SM," Theresa explained. "It's nice. It has air-con." I had no complaints about air-conditioning. Iloilo was hot and stuffy compared to the cool Baguio mountain air. "Here," she gestured. "Dis is a good place."

We sat down at the wood slatted tables inside Mang Inasal, a fast-food chain restaurant found all over the Philippines. Mang Inasal was one of my favorite eateries. I frequented it because they had the best barbecue chicken, and it was quick and affordable on a Peace Corps budget. They also served unlimited rice, which was a huge draw in the Philippines. I knew someone who once ate ten scoops of refills in one sitting. He was a real champ. Either that or he was hungry.

When I was full on rice and chicken, Theresa returned to the table clutching a tray of *halo-halo* goblets. Her face smiled brightly. "You eat, hah. It's halo-halo."

Halo-halo is a Filipino dessert which means "mix-mix." It consists of a medley of sliced fruit, beans, corn, tapioca pearls, jellied chunks, globs of *ube* jam (purple yam jam), a slice of *leche* flan, and ice cream. All of that is thrown together into a bowl of shaved ice then covered in evaporated milk, which is poured over like gushing lava. I had eaten it on several occasions before the Philippines, so the colorful swirl of ingredients was a welcome treat to me. "You eat more, hah," Theresa urged me. I spooned more purple slush into my mouth.

After lunch, my eager travel companions took me to the first stop of the tour—Valeria Street. I stood on the newly paved sidewalk looking up and down the street overpopulated by jeepneys. I squinted at another SM Mall, caught my reflection in a shiny glass high-rise, and noted the chain restaurants and fancy new banks. I tried to imagine what it had looked like almost fifty years ago when my dad was growing up in a small house right where that mega mall now stood.

"Everything is different now," Hanna, my dad's other cousin, explained to me. "Da city is bigger, more developed, more crowded, more polluted." Her soft brown eyes glanced at the industrial scene before us. Exhaust fumes mixed with the smell of McDonald's. I couldn't help but think how this looked like every other street in the Philippines.

Next we drove into the countryside where we toured several of the historic churches in the area: Tigbauan, Guimbal, and Miagao, which is a UNESCO World Heritage Site. Despite my romantic visions of contemplative solitary wandering, it had been a good day after all, and I was thankful for my relatives escorting me to the different sites instead of having to spend hours figuring out which jeepney to take to each landmark.

"Here. I bought *sinigwelas*," Theresa said after we had stopped at a street stand. We all got into the car and snacked on the plum-like fruit.

"Here. I bought you Coke too," she said as she handed me a plastic bag of soda with a flimsy straw.

"Uh, thanks." I took the plastic soda bag and smiled back at her while I sipped. During the trip home, I noticed the familiar pains in my stomach that every traveler dreads. I could feel my stomach muscles cramping up and moving on their own accord. If I could just make it back to the hotel where I was staying tonight, I would be fine. But unfortunately, we still had some time until we reached the city central. Too embarrassed to say anything about my predicament, I tried my best to nod along to the conversation in the swaying car. But my mind was elsewhere, struggling to keep my stomach from moving around too angrily. Although I was used to this kind of situation by now—my stomach had disagreed with me during the most inopportune times in the past few months—it didn't make it any easier.

We finally pulled up to my hotel, and I made my round of goodbyes as quick as Filipino hospitality would allow.

"We hope you enjoyed yourself today! We must hab dinner again dis week, hah," Theresa said enthusiastically.

"Thank you so much for taking me around to visit the churches!" I told them, trying to wrap up the conversation and get on my way. When I finally managed to disentangle myself from my relatives' goodbyes, I checked into my hotel, raced to my room, threw down my bag, and ran to the bathroom. My butt cheeks squeezed together as tight as they could, but just as I reached the threshold of the CR, they suddenly released. I made it to the toilet, but the explosion had soiled some of my clothes in the meantime. *Hay naku! Why, Philippines, why?! Why do you treat me so?* It wasn't the first time this happened, and it wouldn't be the last. It was just a part of living in a foreign country.

~~~

After touring Iloilo with my relatives (without any more accidents), I took a side trip to the island of Guimaras to meet some volunteers for the famous mango festival. The mangoes in Guimaras were of a special variety and boasted sweet, melt-in-your-mouth, dripping-with-juice goodness—the best I had tasted so far in the Philippines. They were so good I even joined a mango-eating contest, which was probably not the best idea for my battered stomach. But the subsequent tummy ache was worth it. Guimaras mangoes were wonderful.

By the time I returned to Iloilo on the ferry boat, I had less than half a day left before I had to catch my flight, but there was still one more place I needed to see. I scanned the roadside signs through the open windows of the jeepney, hoping my relatives' directions had been accurate. Finally, I located the landmark I was searching for and called out "Para! Stop!" to the driver, and he pulled over to the side of the road.

Stepping off the jeepney, the school's white-columned building towered above me. *Is this the one?* I wandered tentatively through the front lawns, not quite sure if I should be excited yet. *Perhaps this is not even the school after all.* It was summer, so students were not to be found. Muted echoes from a loudspeaker emitting from one of the main halls hinted of a conference taking place inside the campus. After loitering around the back of the building, I snuck inside one of the doors and found myself in a black-and-white checkered corridor with whitewashed walls. Around one corner was the Account and Records Office. On a whim, I walked up to the window and asked the woman if she could look up some records.

"It should be around the school year 1963 or 1964," I told her.

Five minutes later she waved at me from behind the glass. "Yes ma'am, here are his records," she said, holding a stack of papers in her hand. In faded typed lettering, my dad's name was printed on the school registration page.

"Can I have this?" I asked.

"No, ma'am."

She was not allowed to release any of my dad's high school records, not even for a payment. But it didn't matter. I had gotten all the information I needed. As I scanned the school grounds, I tried to picture what the place would have been like in my father's day. How strange it was that so many years later I was standing in the same exact place he used to walk every day. This was where he studied. This was where he hung out with friends.

~~~

"That was the same church I had my first communion," my dad told me later when I sent him pictures of my trip. I had gone to Mass at the Jaro Cathedral by chance. It just happened to be the closest church to me that day.

"I also visited the public market with Theresa and Hanna," I told him. "Dad, do you remember those snacks we used to eat when I was little? The banana chips with a brown sugar glaze, wrapped in white paper cones. I found those in the market. They're called *pinasugbo*. I hadn't been able to find them anywhere in the Philippines until I came to Iloilo. They're an Iloilo specialty." As a young child, I remember getting packs of pinasugbo, *pastillas*, and other sweets when my relatives would bring back giant boxes from their yearly trip to the Philippines.

~~~

"Where did you come from? Why were you in Iloilo?" were the recurring questions I got from everyone when I returned. Iloilo City was not exactly a popular tourist destination.

"Your father is from Iloilo? Do you speak Ilongo?"

"No, just Tagalog."

"You must learn Ilongo."

"I'm already trying to learn Tagalog and Ilocano."

"But you must learn Ilongo too."

"Yeah, I should learn Ilongo too," I added, if only to humor them.

I traveled to Iloilo because I wanted to immerse myself in the city where my father grew up. But secretly, I had also hoped to uncover that "aha!" moment in which I would finally understand who I was, or at least where I came from. I departed Iloilo with an ambivalent sense of both accomplishment and disappointment. I had learned a little about my dad's past—I saw the city, the houses, the market, the people—but a lot had changed in the fifty or so years since he had lived there. And the city was also similar to every other Filipino city I had visited. Too much time and distance kept me out of grasp from the past I sought to illuminate. How could I attempt to understand something that would never exist in my time? What was I looking for exactly? I wasn't satisfied with the outcome of my exploration. It was like I had touched the past but didn't understand it. I was just an observer, a visitor, a foreigner. The foreigner who didn't quite belong.

~~~

"Ate came back." I looked up when I overheard the remark. I had just arrived back home from Iloilo, and a crowd of neighborhood men lounged outside my house, chewing *momma* tobacco, drinking gin, and sitting on empty tin paint cans. It was one of the younger tambay men who had spoken.

"Where did you come from, Ate?" another addressed to me. I had never paid much attention to any of them before. I only recognized them by face. *Were they surprised I came back?* I was surprised they even knew I had been gone.

"Just vacation," I answered. Even strangers and acquaintances seemed familiar with my business. But I should have expected that. I was the foreigner after all. And yet, they *had* noticed my absence, which meant that I had presence. I belonged, in some sense of the word.

## 17

# YOU'RE SO FILIPINO

When the wind blew through the mountain canyons and valleys, it always carried with it a distinct scent of fresh outdoor air. The rush of coolness jilted the senses and brought with it a sense of contentment and adventure—I looked forward to exploring more of the Cordillera region in which I lived. The Cordillera mountain region had six provinces, each with their own unique culture and style. My first experience venturing out of my own province of Benguet to other mountain provinces was to Sagada, a town famous for its hiking and caving expeditions.

"Let's go to Sagada this weekend!" Crystal, a fellow volunteer, texted me.

"OK. Sounds awesome!" I replied. I packed my bags, and we left the next day.

As we tumbled down the one-lane highway in an open-air, non-shock-absorbent bus, I popped an anti-nausea pill in my mouth in preparation for the journey. With five hours ahead of me, I passed the time gazing at the awe-inspiring scenery and chatted with Crystal. Cue the country music soundtrack in the background. Mountains upon mountains unfolded before us. Sometimes we drove on a road high above the clouds, and we'd peer down at the hills far beneath us. I watched the clouds as they drifted below, pensive and melancholy, through dipping valleys, crossing vegetable terraces stretching upward.

Crystal pulled out a bag of snacks. "Pandesal?"

"That's OK, I brought some snacks of my own." I pulled out a plastic bag with boiled sweet potatoes inside. "*Kamote?*" I offered.

"Oh my gosh, you're *so* Filipino!" she teased.

"What? Whatever. Sweet potatoes are good! They make a good snack," I tried to protest. She just laughed even more. Crystal and I were both Filipino Americans and frequently joked about being "too Filipino." I wasn't sure how she felt about it, but for me, being *too Filipino* was both an insult and a compliment. On the one hand it meant I was assimilating, but on the other hand it meant I was doing the very things I had made fun of when first introduced to the Philippines and its many strange cultural customs. The paradox of being too Filipino was all too evident to me, but it was still a complex feeling I couldn't shake.

"*You're* so Filipino too with your pandesal bread," I retorted with a smirk.

On my other side, an older man sat in an aisle seat because all the bus seats were already occupied. An aisle seat was a simple plastic seat that flipped down, extending each row for one more passenger. *There's always room for one more*, I joked to myself.

"Are you girls Thai?" he asked curiously.

We both giggled and gave each other a knowing glance. We got these questions all the time.

"No, we're American," I replied. It was not the first time someone had guessed incorrectly at my ethnicity. My tan skin and dark hair suggested many cultural backgrounds. When I was in Hawaii, I was given the "local" discount. When around

Latinos, they'd try to speak to me in Spanish. When I was in Turkey, they asked if I was Mexican. In China, they asked if I was Indian. And growing up in America, they always asked, "Are you Native American?" I come from a mix of different backgrounds: half Filipino, one-fourth Slovenian (or maybe Austrian, we've never been totally sure), one-eighth Irish, and possibly one-eighth French. With my combined multitude of ethnicities, it was fairly easy to blend in or get mixed up with any culture.

Before the Philippines, and even during many periods of my volunteer service, I identified mostly with being American. I grew up in a typical American household and learned American culture just as well as any other kid on my block. My family and I went on camping trips, used a dishwasher, arranged cheese platters for holidays, and ate pancakes and waffles for breakfast. I owned a stamp collection, a bike, and a plastic red Mickey Mouse lunchbox. With floral saddle-strap stretch pants and a fluorescent baggy T-shirt, I wandered through childhood oblivious to the fact that I looked different from other kids.

In elementary school, our family moved from an apartment to a house, which meant I'd enter second grade with a whole new set of classmates. I remember waiting in the cafeteria line for hot lunch when a girl behind me spoke. "Are you Indian?"

"No." I scrunched my eyebrows at her quizzically.

"Well then, what *are* you?"

"I'm American, duh!" I retorted with a sassy eye roll. However, despite constantly getting asked the what-*are*-you question, I never felt treated differently because of how I looked. And except for the occasional you-look-like-Jasmine-from-Aladdin statements, I never delved into or questioned my diversity or ethnicity. It wasn't until seventh grade that I realized I didn't see myself the way others saw me. I declared to my classmate that I wanted to be Snow White for Halloween, and she simply replied, "You can't be Snow White. Your skin isn't white!"

Even so, in high school, I felt unqualified to apply for Filipino American-based college scholarships. Essay questions usually pertained to topics on how Filipino heritage had shaped the way you were today. I didn't have an answer to that and was certain that I could never win a scholarship with an essay starting with "So...I don't have experience in what it means to be a Filipino..." I didn't belong in the category of Filipino Americans who knew their culture with a close familiarity.

Out of curiosity and for fun, I joined the Filipino American Student Union club during my last year of college. I finally had my first real community of Filipino friends, and I began to learn more about Filipino culture, albeit secondhand. Many of them had learned the culture from their parents or grandparents but most had never experienced living in the Philippines for long periods of time. I had learned about specialty foods, traditional dances, and what "Filipino time" meant. But even after becoming involved in the club, I wasn't comfortable claiming the identity of Filipino American for myself. I still felt that I was simply American.

By the time I joined the Peace Corps, I was excited for a new opportunity to experience something different. I was hungry to serve and do my part in the world. But more selfishly, I longed to learn about myself and my Filipino background in the process. I carried a lingering hope that I might be able to understand a part of me that could never be discovered while in America. Living in the Philippines would be my chance to discover what I had missed out on all those years.

~~~

I turned to my aisle seatmate and held out a sweet potato. "Kamote?" I offered.

"Ah! Da food of da mountains!" he exclaimed. "All you need is a few kamote to keep you full." He pointed out various landmarks to me for the remainder of the bus ride, telling me a story about each one. This was where he went to school. Over there was where his friend lived. That's the third highest mountain in the Philippines. He showed me pictures of his family on his phone. I ate my kamote and thought about the strangeness of this situation, one not likely to occur in America. Mountain curves. Country Music. Kamote and pandesal. Making friends with my aisle seatmate. Welcome to the Philippines. So far my search for understanding my roots had been a wild and crazy journey, but I knew I was making progress. I was still getting used to the culture, and I had a lot of unanswered questions, but those things would come in time. Sometimes, just enjoying the moment and soaking up each experience were the best teachers I had.

My trip to Sagada had been a quick one packed with several expeditions. We took a hike through rice terraces that led to a large waterfall, and another day was spent on a caving tour that left me exhausted, wet, but happy to have gone. On the last day of our trip before we boarded our bus, I visited the Sagada Weaving store, famous for its handwoven artisan products. In the mountain provinces, different colors and patterns of woven fabric represented different tribes or provinces. Sagada had a distinct pattern of stripes, which I admired. I chose a blue-and-white-striped shoulder bag and a purple-and-blue woven makeup bag. These both eventually became my prized possessions and received regular use on each trip I took in the Philippines.

Stepping onto the open-air bus, I again popped an anti-nausea pill into my mouth and prepared for the journey home. My blue Sagada Weaving bag lay at my feet, now stuffed with some of my belongings, and I felt a sense of pride carrying a handwoven bag like many of the other Cordilleran residents I'd observed. You're so Filipino, I thought, this time taking it as a compliment.

## 18

## YOU SHOULD SEEK PROFESSIONAL HELP IF...

It was a blustery, wet evening when Chesa arrived at my door, leaning on a giant umbrella like a cane. She told me something about someone's funeral at so-and-so's house and asked if I would come. *Who? Where?* She insisted on accompanying me there. I was unfamiliar with the family and the lola whose funeral it was, but I still accepted. She guided me up the street and onto a side road I'd never walked before. We ran into some of the neighborhood kids, the ones who hung around outside my house, and they watched me with curiosity, wondering where I was headed.

"Where are you going, Ate?" one of them asked.

"I don't know," I answered.

Still confused, I followed Chesa to a house where I heard voices joined in prayer coming from within. I could just make out the words of the Our Father. Then I heard singing. Chesa took me around the back where we entered the kitchen. A woman was chopping a whole pig into smaller pieces on a cutting board, and pots of simmering dishes covered every available burner and countertop space. A funeral meal in the process.

After introducing myself to the confused woman supervising the kitchen, she motioned for me to enter the living room and join the service. Due to the fierce wind outside, we were in the middle of a brownout—all power had gone out in the area. The living room was dark, except for the glow of candles and the occasional flashlight or cell phone glow as people strained to read the prayers and songs in the darkness. I took an empty seat in the back, right next to a man who had fallen asleep. The prayers and singing continued. The airy whistle of wind outside escalated. I settled into my chair and tried to observe the room. *These lolos and lolas can certainly sing hymns with gusto.*

After the closing song, followed by a sign of the cross, the service ended and everyone gathered around the table, now filled with steaming food. This was a good opportunity for me to pay my respects to the woman laid in the casket. She was dressed in traditional garments—a colorful, handwoven skirt called a *tapis*, and a decorated white blouse. In the mountain regions, women wore a tapis, and men wore a garment wrap called a *bahag*. I had seen this type of dress in cultural performances before and enjoyed watching the traditional dancing. The native music and dance steps told stories of war, hunting, nature, and relationships. Dancers moved gracefully to the steady beating of the *gangsa*, a gong instrument.

I looked down at the woman in the casket, imagining her stepping in rhythm to the gangsa sounds. I noticed the pattern and particular colors in her skirt and knew that she was from the Ifuago region of the Cordilleras, like many others in my neighborhood. But what struck me the most was her face. Her wrinkles and gray hair emitted what I had seen of the mountain women I encountered—strength and resilience.

Looking around the room, I noticed Chesa had left quietly, unable to be found for the remainder of the night. The line at the table finally dwindled, and I managed to get a plate with rice and *lechon baboy*, spit-roasted pig. I meandered around the room, eating and chatting, first with the kid whose house we were in and then with a new friend I'd made, a woman who worked in the health clinic at our community center. By the time I headed home, the growing twilight was beginning to match the dark windows of all the houses in the neighborhood. Still a brownout.

~~~

We were well into the rainy season now. On one particularly soggy day, the rain fell in a heavy downpour all afternoon. By evening, I had already congratulated myself on the decision to stay at home and eat packaged noodles instead of going to town to buy food at the market. It was coming down in buckets, so I was glad to be inside my house instead of making my way home on a jeepney, fighting the elements.

Snuggled in bed, I listened as the storm howled a long, lonely sigh, whipping the trees in a foul mood. It sounded embittered and resentful as it passionately scattered the rain, sending violent sprays aimed at my window. With another wail of anguish, it summoned up all its strength, sending forth a gust of wind, racing at breathless speeds. A metal clash below. The flip-flip-flip of a plastic tarp thumped madly out of control until it slackened and the storm paused to take a breath. Then, heaving once more, wildly foaming at the mouth, it bellowed a mournful, guttural cry. Another metal crash below and the lights went out.

An hour later, I awoke to more blasts of rain and loud banging noises. I got up to check the flooding that was accumulating in several areas of my house. *Hay naku! Water everywhere!* I gathered towels and rags to soak up the puddles—it didn't do much good. The rain pounded against my window, but I just scowled back and curled up underneath my covers, trying to sleep.

I had grown fascinated by the sound of Philippine rain—large drops splattering off the banana leaves, a steady rhythm of vigor, power, and force—but at the same time I always dreaded monsoon season, also known as typhoon season or just plain rainy season. It wasn't that I minded the rain. I had lived in the rainy Northwest region of the US for most of my life. I knew rain. But Philippine rain stood on a whole new level. It wasn't necessarily the fact that I might not see the sun for weeks at a time. It wasn't the raging typhoons that drove through the land in a mad furry. It was more the fact that during the rainy season, I had to resign myself to being constantly wet. Clothes couldn't dry on the line. If they did, a surprise afternoon thunderstorm would soak them straight through, leaving them wetter than after having washed them. Downpours were an expected part of the day, and a smart person would never dare leave the house without an umbrella.

The national highway outside my work office would turn into a brown, rapidly gushing river. Mud and sediment mixed together created a swirling flood of muck. It was like someone spilled brewed coffee and creamer and it rushed furiously downhill on the highway heading toward the coast.

If I leapfrogged across the flooded roadway, bouncing from toe to toe through the rivulets, and my Converse shoes got only half wet, they would proceed to get soaked entirely once I crossed the highway and headed down the hill to my house. That giant hill became a long water slide during heavy storms sending a stale coffee waterfall steadily past me, whisking me along, washing up past my ankles. Whatever clothes didn't get wet from the waterfall would soon be taken care of by the sideways shower of rain. It was inevitable that if you chose to go outside, you would get soaked.

When monsoon season was in full force, it drove me reeling into my house in a flurry of fierce wind and rain. I hid under my three fleece blankets only to reemerge timidly in search of food. During one particularly bad typhoon, strong winds and rain trapped me inside my house for several days. After two days, the electricity went out. *No! Brownout!* After three days, my gas ran out. *Curse you, empty gas container!* I huddled in my candlelit kitchen munching the last of my crackers. I tried to make oatmeal by heating up water over my candle, but it was no use. I swallowed a few bites of soggy oats before I gave up. *Why, Philippines, why?*

After a bit, I got up to wring out the towels sopping up the floodwater. My meager supply of towels was doing little to stop the madness, so I added a few old T-shirts to help soak up the endless water. Then the last of my candles went out. I lay on my bed in the dark, listening to the rain. My stomach growled. *Hay naku!* After that episode, I learned to keep my cupboards well stocked for future emergencies.

During the dark days of rainy season, I'd find myself unmotivated and unwilling to make the trek "all the way into town." Even though it was only twenty minutes away, I'd still find the amount of effort more than I was willing to exert. Especially when my neighborhood was filled with thick, moisture-rich fog, threatening to transform into solid water at any second. Instead of going to town to meet up with friends, I'd end up sitting at home, alone, with many things to do but no desire to do them. To combat my self-inflicted boredom, I'd find new activities that would divert my attention to more productive things besides lying on my bed staring at the wall.

One hobby I started was to plant seeds. I planted zucchini, snow peas, tomatoes, lavender, basil, and mint. Every day I'd go out to check on my plants. Sometimes I'd sit or rather squat low to the ground, Filipino style, and stare at my plants. I'd find some sort of hopeful satisfaction in just watching them. It was as if by keeping vigilant watch I'd somehow get to witness their transformation right there in front of me, or will them to sprout above their soil layers and burst into the sunlight, if there ever was sunlight. I'd sit there for several minutes lost in some nature musings before I'd leave reluctantly to other more mundane activities.

Candy was another downfall of mine during the rainy season. It tempted me all through the day. I'd just be reading innocently on my bed, when suddenly I'd become a possessed monster, raiding the kitchen cabinets for sweets I'd saved from a recent care package. *Oh! Rainy season! How I loathe thee!*

The rainy season also meant an ongoing struggle to fight the persistent invasion of mold growth. It was a battle I had lost all confidence in winning. In fact, mold grew on my furniture faster than my clothes took to dry. It would spread over my desk like a fresh layer of snow. If I wasn't careful, my clothes and shoes would get attacked by mold as well. Many shoes were lost to the mold battle, and I sadly threw them out, swearing to myself that I would get even one day. Eventually, I just gave up. *Just let it be. Let it grow. I don't care anymore.* That is, until I wasn't able to sleep at night because of constant sneezing and a runny nose. My allergies grew worse.

"You might check your house to see if there is anything that could be causing you to have your allergic reaction," a Peace Corps doctor advised me over the phone.

"Ah…yes. I have a good idea of what it is…"

"In the meantime, take some allergy medicine."

After texting several volunteers for tips on battling mold, they all responded with similar answers:

"There is no solution."

"I gave up on that battle."

"I have no idea!"

A Google search elicited several websites. One site listed mold-killing products for sale, all of which were not available in Baguio. Another website advised the use of rubber gloves and a surgical mask. "Oh boy," I groaned. It stated that one way to kill mold is through chemicals such as bleach, which I had tried but it simply grew back. I scanned the page and read that another way to get rid of mold is to remove moisture with a dehumidifier. I laughed at my laptop. *Useless!*

A third website claimed that nothing would prevent mold if there was a constant presence of moisture.

A fourth website displayed a side note suggesting to seek professional help if you live in an environment with too much moisture and the mold continually returns. *Professional help?* Well, so much for that.

The weekend following a four-day typhoon, which left my windows and walls fogged with dripping moisture, I decided that something had to be done. After a careful perusing of aisles at the SM Mega Mall, I came home with Lysol Disinfectant Spray and some sort of product that was supposed to eliminate moisture from the air. They proved to be meager weapons for the magnitude of war raging inside my house. *Useless.*

"I use vinegar," Carmelita told me when she heard of my predicament. "About once a week, we wipe down our walls or furniture with vinegar, and it kills the mold."

"Vinegar? Really?!" I could not believe that the solution was so simple, but I tried it. Armed with a spray bottle of vinegar, I attacked my entire house. Black splotches of mold soon disappeared. After a few weeks, I repeated the process to prevent future growth. While I still had to be careful about certain types of clothes or shoes, such as leather items, I had finally triumphed over the mold. I felt like I should have gotten an award, or at the very least, a certificate. *Volunteer fights off army of mold with her bare hands. Victory!!!*

~~~

Toward the end of the rainy season and a few months into teaching Guitar Club, choir, and rap workshops, I organized a "café-for-a-day." It was meant to be a way for the kids to perform the songs they had been learning in a coffeehouse-style performance, thus eliminating all the fuss and formality that came with a recital. Recitals were boring. Coffeehouses were fun. Kids liked fun. Since most of my students and co-workers had no idea what a coffeehouse performance was supposed to look like, I realized I'd be the one pioneering this new territory. There were Starbucks and other coffee shops in Baguio, but they were frequented only by the wealthy. I didn't know too many people in my community who had ever been to Starbucks.

I tried to give some general direction to my co-workers and students who came to help set up. A large schoolroom served as the café space, thus blackboards served as obligatory wall decorations. Posters for ABCs, days of the week, how to tell time, and tracking attendance were also part of the unavoidable decor.

"Ate Debs, how about the stage?" Jay Ar asked.

"Teacher, where will we put the tables?" Benji and Esteban called out.

"Ate Debs, how will we set up a coffee bar?" Carmelita inquired.

The menu on our bar boasted several varieties of 3-in-1 coffee: NESCAFÉ Original, NESCAFÉ Brown 'N Creamy, NESCAFÉ Creamy White, and NESCAFÉ Vanilla Latte. One parent would cut open the coffee sachet and pour it into a paper cup. Another parent would fill it with hot water to dissolve the mixture and then serve it up to the customer. It was a very classy establishment.

Over thirty kids performed at our café, including some of the SDC boys and Guitar Club students. Esteban's strumming still sounded muted, and Samuel's face still looked like he was about to burst into embarrassed laughter, but they were gloating afterward.

"Good job, guys! You were awesome!" I praised my guitar students and gave them high fives. We raised a mere six hundred pesos from coffee sales, but the next day I took that wad of worn bills to Baguio Music Center.

"What's the cheapest guitar you have?" I asked the salesman.

"Dis one here, da Fernando guitar, is seven hundred pesos."

"I'll take it."

The golden wood Fernando guitar became the Guitar Club's newest addition. Now, instead of one good guitar and one broken one to rotate between six boys, we had two good guitars and one bad one for the rotation. We were making definite progress.

"Did you buy dis, Teacher?"

"No, you boys did. With your coffeehouse performance. This is your guitar. You earned it."

"Really, Teacher? Dis is ours?"

"Yup!"

They all had the "Samuel look" that time.

~~~

In early December, the US Ambassador, Harry Thomas Jr., visited Baguio and was invited to come to my worksite to learn about our music program and hear a special performance given by the Guitar Club. He was ushered in by an entourage of security guards and embassy staff. Samuel looked wide-eyed as usual, Jun Jun sat immobilized by such a large foreign audience, and Esteban and Benji forgot where they were supposed to sit. All the band members fidgeted on their stools in silence as the sound guy adjusted their microphones. I sat on the sidelines discreetly trying to give directions using only facial expressions.

After making hasty hand signals and frantic lip pointing that went unnoticed by the boys, I decided I'd better just let them be. *Bahala na!* It was out of my control.

The boys nodded to each other then began their performance, a simple blues song. Both Samuel and Jun Jun had several bars of improvisational soloing, and I sat with a straight face, fists clenched, watching their fingers intently. The audience clapped cheerfully after each solo, and I relaxed a little. An embassy staff member pulled me aside after the performance and told me that the way the boys looked at each other and nodded to signal a change or ending was just like a real jazz band. "The Ambassador loves jazz bands! We were all very impressed."

I smiled politely and thanked him, but I was scowling on the inside. *If only you saw these boys during practice!* How many times did I tell my boys, "You need to look at each other to know when to end. Make eye contact!" But did they ever listen to me? No. During practice they messed around, forgot to look at each other, and never ended at the same time. Yet, they did all those things perfectly during their performance. Maybe they had learned something after all. I stopped scowling.

"Good job, guys! High five!"

~~~

At the end of the rainy season, I put up a strand of white Christmas lights in my house just so I could make it feel cozier. Every time the neighborhood kids came over they liked to plug them in, turn off all the other lights, and heave in collective sighs of awe.

"Ooooohhh."

One evening, Tala and Chesa came over as I was cooking dinner. Chesa flipped my dining area light switch off, leaving just the dim glow of the Christmas strand. *OK, so I guess I'll just cook my food without light*. But then they exclaimed, "It's like a candlelight dinner! Ate, you sit down here, and we'll be your waiter." So they made me sit down while they served me my dinner.

"Let's roast marshmallows, yeah?" I suggested.

"Like Christmas?" Tala asked.

"Christmas? What do you mean?" I questioned as I brought out some candles.

Tala and Chesa explained how roasting marshmallows was a popular activity for children at Christmastime. We roasted away, delighting in the burnt sugary confections. Then I heard a knock-knock at my door. It was Jayden.

"What are you doing, Ate Debs?" As soon as Jayden entered the room, his eyes widened in the glow of the candles and festive lights. He ran over to me, gave me a big hug, and exclaimed, "Merry Christmas!!!"

"Aww, thanks Jayden. Merry Christmas to you too!"

Jayden searched my laptop, found the Christmas playlist on my iTunes, and soon "Jingle Bells" filled the room. Then he spent the next hour fashioning a colorful Christmas sign to add to the decor. It was the best Christmas party I didn't know I'd thrown.

I did end up throwing a real Christmas party, however, as soon as the holidays began. Christmas breakfast was always a special tradition in my own family, and I tried to replicate that with my neighbors. I made French toast, eggs, cookies, hot chocolate with marshmallows, and steaming French press coffee. Ate Malaya had never eaten French toast before, and she accepted the plate I gave her with a shy smile. I cupped the blue coffee mug Mama Ginny had given me as a present, warmth seeping through my fingers as I watched the neighborhood kids eagerly eating, laughing, and goofing off. They dunked giant handfuls of marshmallows in their cups, which consisted of a ratio of one-part hot chocolate, two-part marshmallow.

"Wow, what's dis? Hot chocolate?"

"Ate Debs, can I have more marshmallows?"

"Me too, Ate Debs. I like marshmallows."

Either the sugar rush or just the natural energy of kids brought on a spontaneous dance performance, and a competition broke out. Jayden, as usual, took over my laptop as the DJ and played The Black Eyed Peas' "Boom Boom Pow" three times in a row. That was followed by seven rounds of Owl City and Carly Rae Jepsen's "Good Time." Then he tossed in "Deck the Halls" for good measure.

"Merry Christmas, Ate Debs!" The kids waved when they eventually left to go play outside.

"Merry Christmas!" I called back.

## 19

## THERE'S ALWAYS ROOM FOR ONE MORE

The tree outside my veranda was a firefly haven. In the evening, I'd watch the glimmering hint of sparkles as those fairy tale creatures moved gracefully in and out of the foliage. Congregated in a thick, elongated cluster, they blinked in an undulating wave of shimmering lights, as if a strand of white Christmas lights had come alive with dance. Baguio and its gentle mountain life had begun to romance me in unexpected ways.

I loved the little things about the city the best, from the street vendors selling Filipino-style barbecue, fish balls, and grilled corn on a stick, to watching the sun set over the mountain peaks outside my house. At times, I even loved the brightly painted jeepneys spewing thick clouds of black exhaust. I smiled at the jeepney kuyas collecting fares, laughing, and elbowing their buddies with inappropriate jokes or telling the already crowded passengers to make room. There was always room for one more.

"One more!" they'd shout in Ilocano.

"Who's not cooperating?" the older jeepney kuya would bark in his gruff, scratchy voice.

One more passenger would duck into the jeepney and squish into a minuscule space between a mother with a child in her arms and a heavyset man carrying a large sack full of Mr. Chips and Piattos snacks.

There's always room for one more—that seemed to be the unofficial motto for Philippine transportation. I had seen a family of four seated on one motorbike. I had witnessed a family of four seated on one motorbike with a baby in the mother's arms and a blue tank of gas strapped to the back. Then there was the large flatbed truck carrying at least fifteen people sitting on plastic lawn chairs. Or the open-air city bus that fit three passengers to each bench, with twenty more people standing in the aisles. Convenient flip-down aisle seats in some buses made it easier to pack in the most amounts of passengers per square foot. If flip-down seats were already occupied, some buses had space on the roof where men were allowed to ride, clinging to a low railing.

Philippine trikes were sometimes so small that two people could barely fit comfortably inside while one person would ride behind the driver on the motorbike, sidesaddle style, holding onto the metal frame of the roof for support. However, depending on how the trike was built, it was possible to fit a large group of people, bumbling along like a circus car with twenty graceful acrobats clinging in almost impossible fashion to invisible grip holds. The overloaded trike would zoom by, and everyone would laugh and wave as you stared in disbelief. "We do this all the time," their smiles would tell you. Then another trike, laden just the same, would drive by. And another. Suddenly, you felt ridiculous if you weren't talented in fitting into an overcrowded trike. It was a skill indeed.

Just when you thought there wasn't room on the jeepney, someone would scoot over and a spot would appear out of nowhere. Tall or larger-built foreigners would be told to move over and make room for incoming passengers to which they'd respond with a glance at the two or three inches on either side of them followed by the unmistakable look in their eyes saying, "That's impossible! Are you kidding me?!" But the fact was, yes, it was possible. If you were not squished uncomfortably close to the random guy next to you, if your elbows were not digging into his ribs, and the baby in the woman's lap on the other side was not also sitting in your lap, grabbing your hair, there was still room. If there was an inch or two, that was one more person that could catch a ride.

I loved the random things people carried with them on public transportation. Live chickens carried upside down in plastic bags, twenty-pound bags of rice stuffed into the aisle of a jeepney, large taho metal containers, a thick bamboo pole laden with thirty baskets, heavy-duty bags stuffed full of used ready-to-sell ukay-ukay clothing. Once I saw a goat riding in the seat of a trike. Another time, a motorbike passed by carrying a whole roasted pig sitting atop banana leaves.

Vehicles were also great napping spaces. Open-bed trucks flew down the national highway with men asleep in hammocks tied to poles in the back. Parked jeepneys awaiting their turn in line to drive the next load of passengers would pass the time with a nap, sprawled out on the ripped leather front seat. Sometimes there'd be a merchant asleep on a pile of bagged vegetables sitting in a cargo truck.

The best thing about public transportation was how easy it was to get around, if you knew how to use it. Buses and jeepneys would stop at any point along their route to drop off or pick up passengers. The bus conductors would stand in the doorway, lean outside, and call to people on the street the names of the destinations, gesturing fervently to attract passengers.

"Pasay! Pasay!"

"Buendiaaaaa!"

Bus windshields were also usually stuck with various printed or handwritten signs stating cities and common destinations along the route. All you had to do was hail down a bus heading the direction you wanted to go. Better yet, if you weren't sure which bus to take, hail down a bus and ask the driver if he was going where you were going. Not familiar with where you were to get off? The bus conductor would tell you personally when your destination was approaching. And, if you didn't know how to get where you needed to go, you could simply ask a local on the street.

"Ate, where can I ride a jeepney to Makati?"

"Kuya, where is the SM Mall here?"

Once, I wandered the streets of Manila confused and unsure of where I needed to go, trying to locate a bus to Tagaytay. I stopped on the sidewalk in front of a vendor selling shoes and bags.

"Excuse me, kuya. Where can I catch the bus to Tagaytay?"

"Oh! Hmm. I think it's dere," he said, pointing down the street.

"There?" I asked, wanting confirmation.

"Hey, *pare*, come here," he gestured to a friend nearby. "Where is da bus to Tagaytay?"

"Oh, dat's easy. It's just dere," he answered, pointing in the opposite direction down the street.

"Over there?" I asked dubiously.

The friend called over another friend for advice. His friend asked his other friend for input. Soon there were ten people gathered, debating animatedly the best way for me to get to Tagaytay. It was a hilarious situation, but at the same time, I completely trusted that one of them would have the answer. In the end, I got the directions I needed and caught the bus without a problem.

After months of living in the Philippines, I got so used to getting around by asking the ates and kuyas for directions that I forgot about looking that kind of information up on a Google search. Who needed Google when you had the ates and kuyas?

I also learned to travel with a sense of Filipino time. That meant I'd get there when I got there. No use in hurrying or worrying. The best thing about Filipino time was that if you happened to be late, it was OK. Chances are the person you were meeting would be late too. There was always a way to rectify the situation if I needed to redirect my travels or take another form of transportation. Even when things didn't go as planned, I laughed it away. When I found myself in funny or strange dilemmas, I discovered that I was still at ease. I'd even come to expect situations to be out of the ordinary. Things would turn out alright if I kept a cool countenance and took on the situation with a spirit of adventure. *Bahala na! Let the adventure begin.*

While I came to rely heavily on public transportation, it was never really a luxurious or comfortable traveling experience. Especially during the trip home. After a long weekend of traveling, bus rides home usually induced a vulnerable state of mind. My exhaustion would get the better of me, and my emotions would run amok. My trip would be at an end, and the long ride home became a forced time for reflection and daydreaming. I'd be stuck sitting upright on a plastic or fabric-covered seat until my limbs went numb. Then I'd check my cell phone for the time and realize I still had eight or so more hours to go.

On every bus, vendors would jump on the still-moving vehicle and walk up and down the aisle accosting passengers to buy *buko* (coconut) pies, peanuts, or other specialties of the province we were passing through. If I wasn't careful enough to avoid their gaze or if I accidentally looked at what they were selling, they'd sense a potential customer and badger me until I told them off.

On a return trip home to Baguio, we passed through a province where the specialty was buko pie.

"Buko pie, ma'am? It's still hot."

I shook my head and looked away.

"Buko pie, ma'am! Buko. Buko pie! Ate, buko pie! Buy now."

"I don't want it, kuya!"

"Water, ma'am. Water. Ice tea. Coke."

I shook my head again.

"Buko pie, ma'am. Buko pie."

I looked the other direction out the window and grabbed my iPod. My playlist set a reflective mood, and my mind wandered late into the night when the bus rolled into the Baguio terminal. I stumbled home, threw my blue Sagada Weaving bag on the floor, and took stock of the state of disarray that was my house.

Piles of language books, medical supplies, music sheets, and supermarket receipts lay scattered over all available table space. Clothes worn more times than I cared to remember were piled high, draped over chairs, desperately needing to be laundered. I tried to ignore the explosion of mold in a corner of my room underneath the desk. Its radius had been expanding, creeping outward. The ants had declared my kitchen and dining room as their permanent home. A giant cockroach, perched on top of the counter, stared at me as I walked through the door. I got out the can of Raid. *I'll show him who's boss.*

While traveling gave me a thrill of adventure and exploration, being at home provided a sense of complacency. Lazy afternoons were full of nothing but the ordinary, which is what I liked best. Swinging carefree in my hammock, listening to the sounds of daily life in the neighborhood, lounging in my comfy clothing, cooking chicken and ginger soup, washing my clothes. There was something very soothing about watching clothes hanging on the line, swaying gently in the breeze on a sunny afternoon. Their nonchalant attitude said, "Relax and take a break. You've got all afternoon." Maybe it derived from the satisfaction of knowing that a load of laundry was washed and wrung, waiting only for the rays of sun to finish the final drying. "You deserve a nap," they'd tell me.

Chesa and I lounged around one Sunday, doing nothing in particular but snacking on junk food. The afternoon wore on with no indication of the time passing, the hillside surrounded in a complete blanket of Baguio fog. I ripped open another bag of chicharron and we grabbed the chips by the handful, crunching away. I licked the garlic seasoning salt off my fingers. Our guitars lay forgotten on the tiled floor.

"Look! Outside!" I cried as I glanced out the window.

Trails of smoke rose in slow, lazy columns from the houses below. In the twilight sky, rays of sunlight began to pierce the gloom of the fog. Golden and red hues mixed with an eerie rising mist formed together like an abstract watercolor canvas. I flung open the door of my veranda, and the amber colors of the sunset struck our hair, making our faces glow red as if we were standing next to a fire.

"It's so beautiful, no?" I told Chesa.

"Yes, Ate Debs. It's very beautiful."

## 20

## NO, TEACHER. I'M IN DA BAND.

"Yo! Team English! What's up?!" I called out as Jonas walked past. I held out my hand in expectation. He gave a limp high five, but when he turned away, I saw him smile as he scratched the back of his hair and continued talking to his classmate.

I met Jonas during English class. I didn't normally teach English, but occasionally I was asked to be a substitute. I would have to teach long forgotten things like how to use pronouns, adjectives, and prepositions. Apparently, I was the expert on English grammar since I could speak English perfectly. As I stood up at the blackboard, chalk in hand, wondering how I was supposed to teach these guys English grammar when I'm not even great at English grammar, a hand shot up out of the mass of olive green uniforms.

"Yes?" I nodded at Jonas.

"Teacher, where are you from in America?"

"I lived in the Northwest."

"Teacher, is dat near New York?"

"Er, not really. OK, let's get back to those adjectives. Someone give me an adjective for my guitar."

"Heavy!" Jonas called out.

"Big!" Jun Jun yelled as he raised his hand.

"OK, good. Someone give me an adjective for mountains."

"Tall!" Jonas called out again.

"Beautiful!" Elena added.

"Big!" Jun Jun said.

"Hmm." I looked around the room for inspiration. "Someone give me an adjective for Jonas."

"Handsome," Jonas said, then winked at the class. The girls giggled. Some of the boys threw crumpled paper at him.

"OK, guys, that's enough. Let's do an activity instead." I started to hand out papers.

"Teacher, I can do dat," Jonas said as he grabbed the stack of assignments and handed them out for me. Then the classroom grew quiet for a few minutes while they tried to think of English adjectives.

"Jonas, stop bothering Mae Mae! Go sit down," I said in my stern-teacher voice. Quiet once again.

A few minutes later. "Jonas, go sit down! Stop taking Sherwin's notebook."

"But, Teacher, I'm done now."

I looked around the room. Everyone else was either thinking or writing. "Just stay in your seat, Jonas."

Every few minutes he'd be up again, distracting someone else. "Aw, Jonas! Sit down. Sheesh." I could tell he was intelligent and, like most kids who learned quicker than their classmates, became bored. But trying to make him behave was a losing battle. I didn't know how to win this one.

That summer Jonas joined the camp Carmelita had organized. I was one of the camp leaders, and Jonas was assigned to my group with one other boy, a shy but good-natured kid named Johnny Cash. *Nice name.* Johnny Cash didn't seem to comprehend what I was talking about when I mentioned the real Johnny Cash. *Oh well.* Another volunteer from Australia, Joanna, was also a camp leader in our group, and since the only way for all of us to communicate together was to speak English, we dubbed our ragtag group "Team English." You couldn't find a more random assortment of people, and yet the two boys, despite several years' age difference, got along quite well together. Jonas, with his enthusiasm and never-ending energy, was willing to make friends with anyone. Johnny Cash was content to just be included in whatever we did, and though he barely spoke more than a few words during that week, he still had the time of his life.

Our Team English group was required to create a music video for one of the camp sessions. The song we chose was a Tagalog rap called "Dapat Tama" by the famous Filipino rap artist, Gloc-9. We spent the morning on a grassy hillside filming takes and posing with the lone *kalabaw* (water buffalo) who was watching the strange proceedings. Jonas pulled his sweatshirt hood over his head and put on dark sunglasses. Then Johnny Cash copied. They danced to "Dapat Tama" playing on repeat out of a cell phone, mimicking rapper moves and facial expressions. Jonas did jump shots off a hill and Johnny Cash followed. Jonas ran around with crazy kid energy, so did Johnny Cash. I laughed at it all through the lens of my camera.

At night, each group was supposed to cook their own dinner using the supplies provided as a way to build teamwork skills. Our boys were excited by the challenge, so they got right to work. At first, I just observed the hilarity of the situation—they had no clue how to build a fire. Their paltry pile of sticks lay on the ground while they vigorously lit newspaper rolls on fire then laid them on top of the sticks. The flame would die after a few seconds, and this process would repeat. By now, most groups already had a strong blaze going, and there wasn't any space left under the long metal grill for our boys to use. They had to wait until another group had finished, and then scavenge the remains of their leftover fire. That was when Johnny Cash, a bit overenthusiastic about cutting up the vegetables, accidentally cut his finger, and swearing that it didn't hurt, attempted to continue cutting the food. Blood was getting everywhere, and I wondered if we'd even eat dinner that night.

"Johnny Cash! Please go wash your hands. Now!" I henceforth banned him from cutting anything for the rest of the week. Needless to say, we were the last group to finish cooking dinner that night.

The next day, I was determined to set things right. I showed the boys how to build a fire, and within minutes we were the first group to have the flames ready for cooking. As we sat down to eat, I felt vindicated that we were the only ones finished.

"We're first!" I cried to our teammates. They didn't appear phased by their accomplishment, but at least I was proud of their teamwork.

It was after that summer when Jonas joined Guitar Club that I was able to focus his energy on something more constructive than disrupting classmates from getting their work done. "You got that song down perfectly? OK, here's another one," I'd challenge him. His sense of rhythm translated well to the strumming patterns I'd taught him. Sometimes it felt like I couldn't teach him enough. He'd learn a new song then come back the next day and ask for something else to memorize. Hungry for both guitar knowledge and junk food, he became a regular visitor in the office.

"Teacher Debs, can you teach me something new?"

"OK, hmm, let's see…" I scanned music files on my laptop for something he might like.

"What's dis, Teacher?"

"Oh, those are pretzels. They're an American snack. You wanna try it?"

"Yes!"

~~~

In the Philippines, students entered high school right after sixth grade. This meant that for the new school year, my original six Guitar Club boys had graduated, and I would accumulate a new class of eager guitar enthusiasts, which included Jonas and Sherwin. We also had some of the kids from our summer music sessions join us: Kenneth, Josiah, Sebastian, and Rizalyn.

"Teach me something difficult, Teacher!" Kenneth said to me almost every day. "I want to learn something hard."

"But I just taught you something yesterday. Did you practice it?"

"I memorized it, Teacher. Teach me something else."

"Teach me something too, Teacher!" Josiah piped in. He was Kenneth's brother, younger than him by a year. These spirited brothers had both learned to play guitar during one of our summer music classes, and from that moment forward they were unstoppable.

I never could keep up with Kenneth and Josiah and their relentless appetite for music knowledge. I began pointing them toward tutorials online, which taught songs much more difficult than even I could play. That usually satisfied them, even when they couldn't always play along. It was the inspiration of what was possible to learn that sent them into an overabundance of excitement and enthusiasm about learning guitar. They were happy, so I was happy. They came by my office every day, and I taught them "difficult things."

My lunch hour at work transformed into music coaching and tutorials with my more advanced students. I had an unwritten rule with myself that if a student approached my desk asking for music lessons, unless there was some dire emergency or project demanding my attention, then I would put away all to-do tasks and focus on that student. They scarfed music like the plate of rice and adobo they had brought for lunch that day. They absorbed anything I taught them, and now empowered by the escalated learning, they sought even more knowledge with a fueled eagerness.

It was most impressive to me when kids who were not necessarily the most talented were the most motivated to learn and improve. Rizalyn had also participated in the summer guitar class, and she had come to lessons every day hauling her brand new multicolored guitar. She was entering third grade. Given that I had a dozen or so guitar students, I never paid any particular attention to her at the time. In the beginning, all of my guitar students were bad. That was just how a beginner sounded. Everyone had to start somewhere.

It wasn't until the start of the school year that Rizalyn began to get my attention. Still encouraged and inspired by her summer lessons, she decided to join the band I had formed for accompanying the choir that year. I wasn't aware of her decision until I was directing the band where to sit, and she went and sat right with them.

"Rizalyn, aren't you in the choir?"

"No, Teacher. I'm in da band."

*Oh…OK, band it is.* She was proficient with her basic chords, so I let her be in the band.

Two months later, I became frustrated with the band for not bothering to practice their chords. But Rizalyn practiced. Rizalyn memorized the chords.

"See? Rizalyn already memorized the song. You all need to memorize it, hah."

"Yes, Teacher."

She was the youngest member of our band, but in some ways she was the most valuable because of her enthusiasm and determination to improve, earning respect from the older boys despite her meek outer exterior.

After school during Guitar Club, I'd work with all the students who came, but I could never devote much individual attention because of the large number of kids present. Rizalyn came every day, and she practiced by herself or with her friend. She liked to wait until Guitar Club ended and everyone had gone home. Lingering behind with her friend, still sitting patiently, she asked me in her soft whisper of a voice, "Teacher, can you teach me something?"

"OK, Rizalyn." I noticed that she had a natural inclination to music. She could hear when something was not right and learned fastest by ear.

"Rizalyn, you're getting so good!" I complimented her.

"Thank you, Teacher," she answered, barely audible above the din of the school corridor.

Rizalyn also became the youngest member to join the jazz band that we formed later in the year. Along with her, the band consisted of several guitar players: Jonas, Kenneth, Josiah, and a new boy named Tonton. Sebastian and Sherwin used wooden beatboxes as our two drummers. Another addition to the group was Mikky, our bass player. Mikky didn't know how to play bass; neither did I. But I was familiar enough with stringed instruments to teach him the basic notes and a simple baseline that he could follow. Thus, our first jazz band was formed.

Kenneth was the lead guitarist. He did the solos. He hated playing chords, and playing the melody was much more "difficult" anyway. Jonas became our rhythm leader. Tonton, the other guitarist, followed along to his example. Mikky became the first boy at his school who could play bass. He knew three bass lines. Rizalyn was the one who practiced the most. We also had an unofficial member of our band, Marcos, who was even younger than Rizalyn. He came to Guitar Club one afternoon when the jazz band members were practicing. He was looking like he felt left out, so I taught him a few chords. From then on, he assumed he was part of the "Jazz Rockers," as I called the band. Although he couldn't play the songs, he just strummed along playing the "A" chord for the entire song. I let him "play along" during practices because his smile shone when he played with the "big kids."

"Teacher, will we have Jazz Rockers practice today?" Kenneth asked as he walked into the office.

"Yes! And I have a new solo for you."

"Is it difficult, Teacher?"

"Very difficult."

"Yes!" Kenneth exploded and ran out past Jonas just sauntering in.

"Team English! What's up?!" I gave him a high five.

"Teacher, can you teach me something new?"

"Of course!" I reached for the guitars next to my desk.

"Teacher?"

"Yes?"

"Do you have more of da...prezals?"

"Pretzels? Why, yes I do."

## 21

# HELLO, MESTIZA

"*Mestiza*! Hello, mestiza!" a high-pitched voice of a three-year old girl called out to me from behind the chicken wire covering the sari-sari store window. I peered between the hanging sachets of NESCAFÉ coffee and packets of Tide laundry detergent. Mariella stood on a chair, smiling and waving.

"Hi, Mari!" I called back, trying to match her enthusiasm.

It had been several weeks since Mariella's family moved into the house below mine and took over management of the sari-sari store. Ate Malaya had already left the storefront, having decided to move to Singapore on a work abroad program.

"I'm bored with my life," Ate Malaya confided to me one day. "I want to go somewhere else and do something. To make money." So she left. I couldn't blame her. Anyone who needed to make a substantial amount of money always left the Philippines for work elsewhere.

Every day as I headed off to work, Mariella would recognize me and call out to me. "Mestiza!"

If she didn't see me, I'd call out to her. "Mariella! Mariiii!"

"Mestiza!!!"

I had heard the Spanish word *mestizo* used a few times here before and assumed it meant a Filipino mixed with Spanish blood. I wasn't sure why Mariella's mother taught her to call me a mestizo, or in my case, mestiza. Maybe she had mistaken me for one of the Filipinos in the south, the ones with lighter skin, who descended from mixed Spanish and Filipino families. I observed them a lot in movies and commercials. Apparently, light skin was desirable in the Philippines entertainment business. I wasn't Spanish, but at that point I was used to being called a variety of different names and ethnicities—most of which were incorrect.

"What's my name?" I asked Mariella one day.

"Mestiza."

"Ate Debs. My name is Ate Debs."

"Mestiza!"

"No, Ate. Ate Debs."

"Mestiza?"

"OK, fine. Mestiza."

"Mestiza! Chocolate!"

"Oh, you want chocolate, eh?" Mariella liked chocolate and any other sweets I handed her when she came by my door.

I wasn't fond of her nickname for me. Even if she did assuage me with her cuteness, I often wondered why I couldn't simply be known by who I was as a person as opposed to an ethnic or racial identity. Before moving to the Philippines, I felt uncomfortable claiming the name Filipino or even Filipino American. Why claim something that I knew nothing about? I associated myself with the dominant American culture and skirted any confusion by telling people I was *part* Filipino or that I had Filipino ethnicity. In America's melting pot, that could pass for a satisfactory answer. But in the Philippines, where nationality and ethnicity were one and the same, people defined me as they saw fit.

"She's *only* half American."

"She's English."

"She's a mestiza."

"So, you're half-half?"

"Look! There goes the Americana!"

"She's a foreigner."

There were times when Filipino strangers assumed that I was a local Filipino. Once, I was riding the jeepney in downtown Baguio with a fellow volunteer, and an elderly man kept gazing at us with an obnoxious stare. I stared back. He didn't notice. He was too busy looking at my friend Chelsea's light skin, blue eyes, and long light-colored hair. The "typical American" look. Chelsea was too busy ruffling through her coin purse for jeepney fare to notice him.

"Welcome to the da Pilippines!" he waved and made eye contact with Chelsea.

She looked up. "Thanks?"

"Where you travel to?"

"Oh, we live here. We're volunteers," Chelsea informed him as she handed our fare to the driver up front.

"Oh, bolunteers, eh?"

"Yeah, Peace Corps," I interjected.

"What is your bolunteer organization?" he asked.

"Peace Corps," Chelsea responded.

"Ah! I have heard of da Peace Corps."

"Yeah, we're volunteers from America," I added.

"Peace Corps. That is American, no?" he asked Chelsea.

"Yes," she smirked, noticing the trend in this conversation.

"And where you from in America?" he asked.

"Florida," Chelsea responded, and then looked to me for my response.

"And I'm from…" I began.

"Just be careful now when you are on the streets," the old man continued. "Always stay with her," pointing to me with his lips. "She'll protect you. She'll jump in front of you if someone tries to attack you."

Chelsea and I looked at each other and burst out laughing. Besides being volunteered to jump in harm's way for my friend, my skin color and looks suggested that I didn't need any protection on the streets. Pegged as the Filipino bodyguard? Maybe.

"Actually, I'm American too," I said. "I'm also a Peace Corps volunteer."

"Oh! Excuse me, I thought you were Pilipino," he said surprised.

"Well…I am. Umm…I'm Filam."

"Oh, so you are half Pilipino, half American."

"No. Actually, I'm full American. I was born in America," I replied with great enunciation. He didn't seem convinced.

*I'm American, really!*

Our destination came up on the right. We jumped out the back of the jeepney then turned to look at each other.

"Wow, did he really just say that?" I was incredulous.

"Yup. Guess you better jump in front of me if someone tries to attack me."

"Ha, ha. Funny."

Being mistaken for being Filipino did have its advantages. It meant that I could occasionally escape from the jaw dropping and staring that other volunteers got on a regular basis. But I paid for it in other ways. "She learned to speak Tagalog faster because she's part Filipino," some would say. "Of course she speaks the language better. She has Filipino blood," others would often remark. As if the Filipino gene would automatically help recall Tagalog words before one had even learned them. And while I was hoping to be recognized as a local and not just a tourist or visitor, I was also proud of being American. I wished people could recognize both the American and Filipino aspects of me without referring to me as half-half.

On one occasion, while having a few volunteers stay at my house for the weekend, I even experienced feeling invisible to someone in my own neighborhood. At first, everyone stared at us as we walked up the hill. "We can catch a jeepney right at the top," I explained to them. Two neighborhood boys, who always called out their friendly "Hello, Ate Debs" greetings, were silent as we passed them. Only their eyes moved, following our path. Halfway up, my landlord peeked out from the shadow of her doorway. I waved. She stood transfixed as she watched me accompany my friends up the street. I was used to some staring, but today they were even more obvious. One foreigner who looks Filipino is not as exciting as three foreigners all together. Then an older man approached us with a goofy grin on his face not even trying to hide his awestruck look of delight. I knew what was coming.

"Hello, sir!" he addressed my friend Munya, an African American guy with a bellowing laugh that set anyone at ease. The wrinkly man's eyes bulged, and his mouth hung agape as he extended his hand in greeting. Celebrity Munya and the awestruck man exchanged handshakes and greetings. Then he extended his hand out to my friend Chelsea.

"And who are you, ma'am?"

She introduced herself, and they both explained about being Peace Corps volunteers. I waited for Awestruck Man to move down the line and ask my name as well.

"Welcome to da Pilippines!" he exclaimed to both of them, then headed on his way. I stood there shocked.

"Well, I guess he doesn't want to meet me!" I said in mock offense.

"That's because you're not *pure American*," Munya teased. He knew that term annoyed me.

"Whatever."

I was used to hearing an assortment of contradictory comments about my lack of American looks or she's-obviously-a-foreigner looks. My inability to speak or act Filipino. My mixed ethnicities, which puzzled people. I didn't fit into their box. I was not a blonde American. I was not a returning *balikbayan*—a Filipino living abroad who came back to the Philippines, the land of their birth. I was something else.

These types of experiences and comments happened almost daily, causing an identity crisis that sent me spinning in confusion. Greeted with "hello, mestiza" every time I walked down my street was a constant reminder. There were times when I could ignore the annoyances, but I grew tired of people making assumptions about me. I could no longer avoid confrontation with my identity. I resolved to make a better effort to understand who I was and how I fit into this place.

"Why does Mariella always call me mestiza?" I complained to Munya and Chelsea one evening.

"Isn't that your name?" Munya joked as he served himself some pancit noodles. "Where's your salt?"

"I mean, I'm not Spanish or anything." I handed him an empty coffee tin where I stored my salt.

"This is where you keep your salt? You're so Filipino," he teased.

"What? I like to reuse things."

"Yeah, that's why I said you're so Filipino."

"Whatever."

I decided to investigate my mestiza nickname. A simple internet search provided much needed insight. In the Philippines, the term mestizo refers to a person who is mixed Filipino and foreign ethnicity. *Ah, now everything makes sense.* I now realized how Mariella's family saw me—half-half. Half Filipino, half foreigner. The "foreigner" thing still aggravated me though. *Was I not Filipino? Why do I always have to be a half of something? I've been living here for so long now. Do I not belong?*

In my mind, I could articulate what I was in the negative sense—I knew what I was *not*. I wasn't *just* Filipino. I wasn't *only* half American. I wasn't a white American. I wasn't a pure American, whatever that meant. When others pointed and called me American, I resented them. If they pegged me as Filipino, I would insist I was American. If they said I was Filam, I'd feel as if I was only two halves that didn't equal a whole. If Filipinos defined me as mestiza, I'd feel like I was a foreigner who didn't belong. *I mean, seriously, what was I?*

To an outsider it may have seemed a trivial problem—why not just call myself both Filipino and American? But to me, it was a complex mass of factors that were often contradictory. Identifying with a culture meant more than just using a name. It involved acceptance, belonging, knowledge, confidence, self-assuredness—all things I had not found here yet. That paradoxical tension between my Filipino and American identities was eating away at me, continually resurfacing without a resolution. I just couldn't make sense of it. I felt caught somewhere in the middle. I was neither Filipino nor American. Just mestiza.

## 22

# OFW

"We left Iloilo a little before dark I guess, five or six, somewhere around there," my dad recounted. "We got to Manila just before sunrise so we could see the Manila harbor lights, but I didn't see much of anything because it was night. My mom was like, 'Go to sleep!' But I couldn't sleep. I'd sleep for about an hour and then I'd wake up and try to see where we were. You can't see anything," he laughed. "It's dark."

I had asked my dad to tell me more about our family history—after living in the Philippines, I realized just how little I knew about my Filipino relatives. He continued on, recalling his experience of leaving the Philippines. "It was the first time I left Iloilo, for good! I thought, 'OK…I won't come back here.' And so then we went to Manila, and that was the first time I had been there. My impression of the harbor: Wow! So big! So many buildings, so many lights!

"We went to the airport and then I look out the window and here's this huge airplane, Boeing 707, and it's really long. Wow! That thing can fly? It's so big, right? And inside the airplane, when it was flying I thought, holy mackerel, what is going on?! And you have this adrenaline combination of being scared and being excited at the same time. But I was impressed with this jet airplane…I could actually walk inside the airplane."

My dad explained that his father was an Overseas Filipino Worker (OFW) starting in the 1950s. When my dad was about six years old, his father left the Philippines to work in Guam at the US military base.

"Your lolo was a teacher by trade, teaching elementary students. At the time, the US was looking for workers to go to Guam because Guam was being set up by the US as a military base. So he signed up to work in Guam on a two-year contract."

My lolo would send money home each month from his paycheck, and after two years he was able to come home to visit. Workers who chose to sign up for another two-year contract were given a month of home leave as well as paid airfare. My lolo continued to renew his contract every two years. He worked on the base for ten years, after which he was able to apply for US citizenship. Then he applied for each of his family members—his wife and his three sons.

My dad, the first of his family to join my lolo, was sixteen when he left the Philippines. Two years after he lived in Guam with his father, the rest of the family was finally able to join them. Then, after graduation, my dad went to study in Hawaii and stayed in the US permanently. His brother graduated from high school then served a one-year internship at the naval shipyard in Guam in order to gain a scholarship for college in the US. His other brother studied in Guam and then got a job with the local government.

"At what point did Lolo and Lola come to the US?" I asked.

"Well Lolo, he retired at sixty-five from the naval base, and then he stayed in Guam for about a year. This is where my memory is a little blurry. I think he had a little stroke when he was still in Guam after he retired. He decided to move to the Philippines. He bought a property in the Philippines, in Jaro, and built a house there. So they lived there for about a year maybe. And then what happened is my mother had asthma, that you inherited from her, and her asthma started getting worse and worse, so her doctor said, 'You need to get out of the Philippines.'"

Philippine air was not great for anyone, especially if you had any kind of lung condition. Not desiring to return to Guam, my lolo and lola left instead for the States and lived with my aunt and uncle before they found their own apartment and settled there.

~~~

"Chesa and Charlene are leaving."

I heard this one night from Jayden as he sifted through my iTunes, playing DJ as I cooked dinner. "This weekend," he said. *This weekend?!*

I'd been expecting this for some time. Chesa told me recently that her mom would be arriving soon from abroad and would be taking them back with her to Canada. Still, Jayden's declaration was jolting news to me. *Who's going to knock on my door every day asking for guitar lessons now?*

The next day, I printed out several pictures as a remembrance for Chesa and Charlene. Tala flipped through the photographs I had printed, and while browsing she asked, "Will you miss them, Ate?"

"Of course!" I answered. After a pause, "I'll miss you too…I'm going to miss all of you."

Suddenly, Jayden burst out, "Merry Christmas, Ate!" then hurled himself at me with a ferocious kid embrace. It wasn't Christmas, but I still gave an "aww" in return.

Almost every family I knew in the Philippines had at least one relative who worked abroad or who wanted to: Ate Malaya, parents I talked with at school, co-workers, and relatives of neighborhood kids. For many families, it was their only option to survive. For young students, it was a way out of the poverty that was the only thing they'd ever known. Often, young people aspired to go to college and get a degree because it would help them go abroad to work. Students were educated, trained, and then left. I often wondered about what would remain if all those who were well educated left the country. What would it mean for the future of the Philippines, a country for whom family life and structure were as much ingrained in the culture as the serving of rice with each meal? OFWs were meant to be a temporary solution, but nowadays, it had become the cultural norm. Would this trend continue?

Ma'am Ligaya's husband worked abroad in Guam to support their family. The last time she saw him was when he came back for Benji's graduation, and before that, it had been two years. "Kung may tiyaga, may nilaga. If there is perseverance, there is a meal on the table," Ma'am Ligaya told me, the same phrase Ate Malaya had quoted to me once before. Every afternoon after work, Ma'am Ligaya departed to buy food at the market, cook dinner, do laundry, clean the house, or take care of home repairs. Occasionally, she did her neighbors' laundry in order to make a little extra money.

"I don't like it when people say that things will always be this way, so why even try," she explained to me. "There are people who like to take shortcuts, but I believe honesty is the best policy."

I admired people like Ma'am Ligaya who could look at her life with hope, recognizing that perseverance and hard work was how you survived. I thought about the families I knew who were separated because it was necessary for one or more members to work abroad. I was conflicted when I thought about Chesa and her sister living and growing up in Canada. On one hand, they now had new economic opportunities they didn't have in the

Philippines. But on the other hand, how much would they miss their life here, the culture, speaking their native tongue, playing with friends who understood them? Would they get homesick? Would they remember the Philippines?

Later in the evening, I went over to visit with Chesa and her family and to say my farewells. I met Chesa's mom who was a few years older than me. She thanked me for teaching Chesa guitar and promised to keep her practicing hard. She told me that she had been saving for the past few years while working in Canada so that she could bring her girls to come live with her.

"Perhaps we might meet again someday," she said. "You must come visit us sometime if you are ever in Canada."

I smiled, then stood up to say goodbye. I left in good spirits but still felt empty inside. Chesa had pushed her way into my life. Trying to set boundaries with a girl like that was like trying to stop the monsoon rain from coming. It just comes. And she just came every day. Despite, or maybe because of, her insistence at coming over every single day, she had become a steady part of my life in the Philippines.

## 23

## MUSIC AND COFFEE

My children's choir had grown. They were still the same rowdy roomful of students, but at least they had become rowdy singing students. I decided I had accomplished my original goal. Create a choir? Check. It was now time to take it to the next level. I had the brilliant idea of forming an a cappella choir. The movie *Pitch Perfect* had just gained popularity in the Philippines, and I was determined that my kids could also make beautiful music using just their voices. I recruited the most eager students.

"Hey, Sebastian, how would you like to be in an a cappella choir?"

"Not really, Teacher."

"Too bad, I'm making you."

"Team English, you like music, don't you?"

"Yes, Teacher."

"OK, how would you like to join our a cappella group? It's just like in *Pitch Perfect*."

"I like dat movie!"

"Yeah? OK, then you're in."

Things got serious when the word spread. The principal at our school loved the idea. A few days later, she came into the office and asked, "Do you want to join an a cappella school district competition?"

"That exists?" I asked.

"Yes, something new this year. They've invited our school to take part in a choir competition. What do you think? Should we join?"

"Why not?" I answered rather confidently. We'd only just formed our a cappella group, but my kids could handle it. I had really enthusiastic students.

Several hours of my Saturdays were now spent on choir competition practice. The song had already been chosen by the competition organizers. Points were awarded for harmony, musicality, and tone. *Harmony? This is a kid's choir competition, right? It's OK, my kids can handle it.*

"Listen to the melody and repeat it," I instructed my newly formed a cappella group. "OK, good. Now here's the harmony part. Listen to the notes and repeat it. OK, good. Now, let's put the two parts together."

The "two parts together" ended up as a new melody somewhere in the middle of the two parts, or morphed into just the melody, or just the harmony part.

"No, not quite. Try it again," I encouraged. They tried again without success.

"No, no, no. Let's try again. Listen to the notes!"

I felt bad for Jonas, who had probably joined just because he liked music and I always gave out merienda snacks.

"OK, Jonas. Listen to me sing the note, and then you match the note exactly." I sang out a pitch. "Aaaa."

"Aaaa," he hummed back in a completely different pitch.

"No, listen. Aaaa."

"Aaaa," he repeated.

"No. That's a different note. Try again. Aaaa."

"Aaaaaaa," he tried again on a different pitch.

"Hmm. Maybe we'll work on that later."

My kids were quite good for their age, but sometimes I got a *little* too passionate about music lessons and demanded too much from them. I had to remind myself that they were just kids, and their dedication to music was not going to be the same as mine. Some days I really had to tell myself to let it go.

Things my evil twin/alter ego would think:

> "What do you mean you'd rather go home than attend jazz band practice?"
> "Just listen to the note and match the pitch! It's not that hard."
> "You have no jeepney fare to get home if you stay for practice? *You* should have thought of that beforehand."
> "Oh, you're going to play computer games this weekend? What about practicing those scales I taught you?!"

Occasionally, when the more advanced students sounded impressive in rehearsal, I'd get excited and have them rehearse the songs even more. They'd grow weary of being forced to concentrate for such a long period, and I'd pay for my greedy enthusiasm with an unofficial practice strike. At that point, stage-mom Ate Debs would realize that it was time to give the kids a break.

It was during this time that I decided to apply for a grant to fund our music program. I bounced ideas off Carmelita and Jocelyn and eventually decided that we could hold coffeehouse performances once a month. The students who participated in the music lessons or choirs would then have a chance to perform at the coffeehouse. Most importantly, we were in dire need of more instruments. So far we had accumulated a meagre inventory of two guitars (one of them mine), an acoustic beatbox (mine too), and a keyboard that didn't play "middle C" and sometimes "F." A grant was definitely needed.

~~~

"How's the grant writing going for your music program?" my friend Ben asked one day. He was also a Peace Corps volunteer who had been placed in Baguio just a few months ago. He rummaged in his pocket for his wallet while I looked at the ice cream flavors behind the glass. We were at our favorite ice cream store on Session Road, the main street running through downtown Baguio.

"Ugh. I still need to do a lot of work on it," I replied. "It looks like we'll go through with the music café idea, but I need to just sit down and get through the proposal." I handed the cashier a few coins and pointed at the ice cream case. "Mango, kuya."

"And chocolate chip cookie dough for me," Ben added, dropping some coins on the counter. We walked up Session Road with our waffle cones, passing a cluster of aunties walking too slow.

"The project sounds cool. Let me know when you need help editing the grant."

"Thanks, Ben! I will."

~~~

Choir competition day had arrived. Stage-mom Ate Debs had worn her students down, and she had learned her lesson. Fun choirs were better than perfect choirs. Positive teachers were better than mean teachers.

"Why is Teacher Debs so *masungit*, mean?" one of my students had asked his homeroom teacher.

"It's because you are so *magulo*, rowdy," she responded.

As we walked into the auditorium for the competition, it turned out that our principal had been misinformed. It was not an a cappella choir competition after all. Every choir present had an accompanist. "Well, that would have been useful information," I murmured. As the competition began, I became scared for my kids. With each group that performed, I realized that our rag-tag a cappella choir was out of its element.

"You're going to do great," I coached my kids with a big smile. My stomach fluttered, and my armpits got sweaty.

The rules stated that the choir directors were not allowed to be onstage with their students. So my students arranged themselves on the stage and then began their song without music accompaniment. I sat in one of the auditorium benches with the teachers and chaperones who had come along. Up on stage, Sherwin, stone-faced and wearing sunglasses, remained in a frozen position for the entire performance. Even when the choreography called for movement or clapping, he was a statue. A statue wearing sunglasses. However, most of the choir members sang their parts well and managed to look like they were having fun.

After the kids finished the performance, they exited the stage, some with large goofy grins, others with paralyzed faces. Most of them hadn't quite registered the fact that they had just undergone a nerve-racking experience of singing in front of a large, intimidating audience. Stage-mom Ate Debs was proud, despite our choir earning record lows in competition scoring.

"We're done! We can celebrate!" I cried out in relief. Then I bought them all ice cream on the way home.

"Teacher Debs, that was fun! When's our next competition?" Mae Mae asked.

Never again, I swore to myself. "Hmm, good question. I'll look into it."

Now that the competition was over, I had more time on my hands again. I spent Saturdays doing regular things like grocery shopping, writing, or hanging out in town with some of my friends. A trendy café called Beanstalk had recently opened in the heart of Baguio, and Ben and I frequented it on the weekends.

One afternoon, we were lounging at a table there with our laptops out, making use of the free Wi-Fi. "Hey Ben, wanna help me edit my grant?" I asked. "I'm finished with the draft."

"Sure, no problem. Let's see what you have."

I pushed my laptop toward him and sipped away at my latte while he read through the proposal. Looking around at the café decor and environment, I tried to envision what our own music café would be like. We were planning on doing a pop-up café just once a month in the same schoolrooms we had used before. But the idea of it simmered in my mind. I liked the taste of it; I liked how the idea made me come alive. *My kids are going to love it.* And that made me smile. For months now, I had been looking for a meaningful purpose at work, hoping to feel useful as a volunteer. Helping bring this program to reality had given me the purpose I needed.

~~~

Just one month before the anticipated start of the new music café program, we received the funds we had applied for from a Peace Corp partnership grant. I felt like a baller ready to drop those peso bills as I walked through the mall department store, clerks jumping to attention at our entourage of shopping carts, teachers, and gangly teenagers. I decided to turn the trip into a game. Each group of students had a list of items we needed; their task was to locate and select each item.

"Teacher Debs, are these cups nice?" Mae Mae asked.

"Ate Debs, how about the trays? How many?" Carmelita called out.

Towels, aprons, teaspoons, and dessert plates filled the baskets. Items were crossed off the list. Coffeemakers, electric tea kettles, espresso glasses. When everything had been gathered, assembled, and purchased, we moved on to the music store. Guitars, beatboxes, shakers, microphones, cords—it was any music lover's dream to buy so much equipment at one time. The store clerk gleefully packed everything in bags and boxes, bewildered at his own good luck on such a sale.

A few days later, I walked from the market back to the jeepney terminal carrying several bags of groceries.

"Hello, Ma'am Debs," a voiced called out.

I turned around at the sound of my name. It was a quiet but familiar voice. "Khyle!" I exclaimed when I recognized him. "How are you?"

"I'm good, Ma'am Debs. I graduated already."

"Wow, that's so great!" Several men pushed carts of potatoes past us. We stood at the edge of the market.

"Iiiirisan! Iiiirisan!!!" a jeepney conductor yelled out, notifying everyone in the vicinity of the departing jeepneys nearby.

"I heard you were on a rap competition on TV. One of my students said she saw you perform."

"Oh, yes, Ma'am Debs. But I didn't win."

"I'm sure you did great."

"Thanks, Ma'am Debs. Good to see you! OK, bye now."

"Wait, Khyle. You should come perform at our new music café. We will have a grand opening next month."

"OK, Ma'am Debs! I'll come."

"Take care, Khyle!"

Only two weeks remained until opening day. While the original vision of the music café was to provide free music classes and a performance venue to students in my community, we had also decided to create an opportunity for youth to join a food-service training program. The café server trainees we had recruited from fifth and sixth grade had serious, concentrated faces as they walked the length of our school canteen, tray in hand, practicing balancing dishes and pretend food items.

"Like dis, Teacher?"

"Yes, Elena. Very good."

They were very enthusiastic trainees. Maybe a little overenthusiastic. "Careful, Mae Mae!! Don't run with a tray of coffee glasses," I warned.

Joanna, the volunteer from Australia, helped train a few parents on how to run the espresso machine and make lattes, cappuccinos, and mochas. It was the first time many of them had tried an espresso drink.

"Wow, *sosyal!*" some mothers commented when they got to taste their creations. Sosyal was an expression that meant something was top-notch or fancy—something a wealthy person might be used to. Buying an actual espresso drink in town at Starbucks would cost about one hundred and fifty pesos. That's more expensive than what an average dinner would cost at a hundred and twenty pesos—the drinks at our café *were* sosyal. Of course, since we weren't Starbucks and we ran our café with volunteers, we planned to charge significantly less for our espresso drinks.

On the day of the café opening, I walked into the schoolroom where we had everything set up. The stage backdrop hung with the smell of freshly printed tarpaulin. The banner read "Inspiring Change through Music." Some men were setting up tables and sound equipment. Carmelita and Jocelyn stood at the coffee bar arranging cookies.

"Almost time now, Ate Debs!" Jocelyn said.

"Yes, almost time." I smiled.

Soon, the walkway outside the classroom began filling with students and parents. A big ribbon had been tied to the doorway, and the director of the school and community center made his way through the crowd toward the door.

When the time had finally come, the director proclaimed, "The music café is now officially open," and he cut the ceremonial ribbon. The crowd cheered and applauded. Mothers blushed and giggled as I tried to take their picture. Guitar Club members scrambled to collect their music and practice before their performance.

"Are you ready to perform, Rizalyn?" I asked as she stood next to me clutching her music book.

"Yes, Teacher."

"Are you nervous?"

"Yes, Teacher."

"Don't be nervous. You are very good now."

"Thank you, Teacher."

While the café tables filled up with families from the school, I scanned the crowd for my former students who I had hoped would come.

"Teacher, do you have the chords for 'Orange Sky?'" Team English asked.

"You don't have your copy?"

"No, Teacher."

"OK, try to find another copy." I handed him a stack of books and music sheets. "Mae Mae! Maria!" I called across the room. The two eager girls ran over.

"Yes, Teacher?"

"Go call all the choir members. Tell them the choir will be performing first."

"Yes, Teacher."

Johnny Cash arrived with his country-guitar-playing friend, Jhimmy, who had helped us teach guitar lessons last summer.

People always cheered when Jhimmy played and sang. His voice vibrated with a natural country twang, and he amused audiences with classic rock and country tunes. Then Samuel and Jun Jun sauntered in; Samuel still wore his usual smirk.

"Samuel! Jun Jun! You came!"

"Hello, Teacher."

"You're both going to perform, right?"

"Yeah, Teacher."

"Where is Esteban?"

"He's coming, Teacher."

Team English was back at my side. "Teacher, I will perform 'Huling Sayaw' with you, no?"

"Yes, we practiced it."

"Can we practice it again?"

"OK, one more time. Where is your music?"

"I forgot it at home, Teacher."

"Oh, fine. I'll find my copy."

"Wait, I think I have it memorized now, Teacher."

I noticed Kenneth and Josiah inspecting the guitars off to the side of the stage. "Teacher, can you teach me something difficult?" Kenneth asked.

"Right now?! Go ask your Kuya Jhimmy."

"OK!" He scurried off.

"Teacher, like this?" Rizalyn asked at my other side. She strummed a few chords for me.

"Yes, Rizalyn," I said, distracted.

Kenneth yelled over the rising noise in the room. "Teacher, where is Kuya Jhimmy?"

"He's just over there!" I yelled back. I looked at the clock. *Almost time now.*

"Hello, Ma'am Debs." Khlye and his friend Jayson had slipped into the room.

"Khlye! Jayson! I'm so glad you came! You will perform your rap songs tonight?"

"Yes, ma'am," Khlye answered in his ever polite voice. I beamed at him.

"Teacher, the choir is ready," Mae Mae informed me.

"OK. Here we go then. Let's start!"

I sat at one of the café tables with a few friends who had come to witness our opening night. As I looked around, I felt alive and brimming with excitement. Even though it was just a once-a-month café set up inside an elementary schoolroom, we were classy in our own way. We served espresso drinks, at least. That was a step up from 3-in-1 coffee sachets for sure.

~~~

"We did it, Ate Debs!" Carmelita gushed later that night as we both cleaned up after the performance.

"Yes, we did, didn't we?"

Although it had been a year and a half into my two-year service contract, I felt like I had just begun to make progress. But that was Filipino time. It happened when it happened, I guess. I was just beginning to gain momentum and I wasn't ready to leave it all just yet. When the opportunity came to extend my contract for an additional year, I sent in my forms without a second thought. I was curious to find out how the music program would grow. I still loved teaching my kids and hoped to help them advance further. And, I also needed time for discovering more about myself. Even though I had a sense of belonging in my community, I wanted to understand how I really fit in. I was waiting to see where my journey would take me next.

While I watched family and friends wistfully from afar as they moved about their lives with modern conveniences like cars and hot showers, something else lay in store for my own life. I had chosen a different path for the time being. America could wait.

Things I've learned thus far in the Philippines:

1. Patience is a virtue. I have *some* patience after all, I guess.
2. A guitar is a *very* effective tool for doing useful things.
3. A third year would not be so difficult, would it?
4. *Bahala na!*

## 24

## THE KUYAS AND ATES

On a twelve-hour night bus to the province of Cagayan, I awoke to the noise of our bus conductor shouting at passengers in Ilocano.

*OK, what's going on?* I yawned. *Seriously, it's the middle of the night, kuya. Why are you yelling?* After he finished giving directions, half the passengers got off. The woman in the seat adjacent to mine gathered her things and got off as well. *Uh oh!* I remembered distinctly how she had told the conductor "Tuguegarao" as she handed him her ticket. Tuguegarao is the capital of the Cagayan province, and it was also my stop. I was supposed to meet a friend there for a training the next morning. *Should I get off too? What was going on?*

"Kuya, what happened?" I stood in the bus aisle tapping the conductor's arm. He answered me in Ilocano. *Hmm, not helping.* A polite couple in front of me told me that the bus was having problems, and some people were switching to another bus that was leaving right now. I asked the conductor if I should switch buses. I told him several times, "Tuguegarao." He ignored me because he was too busy giving directions to other passengers.

"Kuya, should I move? Tuguegarao," I repeated once more. He finally nodded yes. I gathered my bag and moved from my nice deluxe bus that didn't make stops to a crappy regular bus that stops for everything: picking up passengers, dropping off passengers, taking rest stops, picking up more passengers, then more rest stops. *Bahala na!*

6:14 a.m. I blinked at a light pink sky, which revealed a small mountain range off to the right. *Where am I? Is this bus really going to Tuguegarao?* I wasn't so sure anymore. I looked around for the woman who was sitting next to me on the previous bus. I couldn't find her in any of the seats.

"Excuse me, Kuya, are we going to Tuguegarao?" I asked as the conductor passed down the aisle.

"No, ma'am. We will not pass Tuguegarao," the conductor said, confirming my suspicions. I cursed the kuya from last night for his awful directions. Or maybe I had just gotten on the wrong bus. *Hay naku!*

I moved up to an empty seat in the very front so I could talk to the driver. I knew that if they dropped me off in a main town, I could catch another bus going the direction I needed. Or, if they just dropped me off on the highway, I could probably hail another bus going to Tuguegarao. Catching buses in the Philippines was no problem. Getting around was not the difficult part. It was just knowing when and where to do it. I depended solely on locals for this kind of advice. It was the only way to know, really.

"Kuya, is there a way to get to Tuguegarao from here?" I leaned toward the driver from my seat. Whenever I got confused or lost, I tended to revert more to English, and this immediately changed the game. It was as if English was the magic word, or words rather. I conversed in Tagalog when I wanted to go undetected, unnoticed, and attract fewer guys who would hit on me. But the moment I blurted out even one sentence in English, I'd have all eyes on me, a few inquiries for my phone number, and often personal service that went the extra mile. One time I was the only passenger left, and the driver kuya personally dropped me off at my destination, which was completely out of the way. English was the best option when I was lost.

"Oh, I thought you were Pilipino," the driver replied.

"I'm half. So…Tuguegarao?" I tried to navigate back to the subject.

"So, you live here? Or travel?" he continued questioning me.

"I live here, in Baguio."

"Do you hab boyfriend? Maybe you hab boyfriend in the States. Do you like Pilipinos?"

"Oh…I'm…married," I laughed. Sometimes it was easier to avoid getting hit on when I told people I was married.

"Don't worry," he finally reassured me. "I tell you when to transfer bus to Tuguegarao." He flashed that kuya grin. Personal service with a smile.

I sat back and tried to get a little more sleep. Seats that were cramped and barely cushioned were not the best for overnight sleeping. Pieces of conversion floated my way as I overheard the conductor and bus driver conversing in Tagalog. I tried to eavesdrop.

"She is an English speaker. From America."

"She's beautiful. Like a celebrity."

"Oh yes, like a celebrity."

I smiled. There I was with messed up bus hair, a less than desirable amount of sleep, teeth unbrushed since last night, wearing a stretched, worn-out T-shirt, and yet they said I looked like a glamorous star. *Oh, kuyas. Oh, Philippines.*

The kuyas were known for their eager, over-helpful attitudes and their inclination to tell you how beautiful you looked. Once in Baguio, I left a coffee shop and crossed the street to call a taxi. Four security-guard kuyas jumped out into the street, hailed a taxi for me, opened the door politely, and bid me farewell.

"Here you go, ma'am."

"Good afternoon, ma'am."

"Take care, ma'am."

It made me smile. *Oh, kuyas. Oh, Philippines.*

The ates, too, were known for ensuring you received the full Filipino hospitality. They ushered you into their houses ("Have you eaten yet?") and made you feel at home ("Here eat dis. You eat more, hah!"). The kuya smile was a welcoming one. The ate embrace made you feel like part of the family. To me, the ates and kuyas embodied Filipino culture. I loved the variety of ates and kuyas I happened to meet while traveling throughout the Philippines, and I loved the wide spectrum of personality types and professions and lack thereof. There were the driver kuyas, the conductor kuyas, the jeepney and trike kuyas. There were the market ates who sold you vegetables. The phone-card ates. The confused-store-clerk ates who could never tell you if their store carried a specific item or not. There were the rowdy-bar-and-videoke kuyas. The beer-drinking kuyas of my neighborhood. The tobacco-spitting kuyas at the bus station. Socks-and-locks kuyas. Glue-and-hairbands ates.

Once while on vacation in Siquijor, some friends and I were out enjoying a fun night of videoke at a bar near our hotel. An enthusiastic kuya offered us shots of Emperador Light Brandy while he bellowed his song into the microphone.

"*Tagay*! Cheers!" he hollered as he lifted his glass to us each time he downed another shot. His oversized basketball jersey hung far below his shorts giving the illusion that he wasn't wearing any pants. We couldn't stop laughing but raised our glasses anyway for a cheer.

"Tagay!" I cheered back as I downed a shot and perused the songbook for a good videoke song.

During an island-hopping adventure in Palawan, some friends and I took a boat tour. A laconic kuya pushed our boat through the water with a bamboo pole, his skin darkened with the unrelenting sun of the Visayan Islands. As we glided into a narrow opening between two steep cliffs, he was poised at the bow; his peaceful stature reflected the mood encircling us. The rhythmic lapping of waves, the long strokes of the bamboo pole. Wind sweeping through the cove, lifting my hair with a playful tease.

When I visited Marinduque for Holy Week to experience their traditional Moriones Festival, I found myself lost, looking for directions to the town's cathedral. An ate nearby learned of my predicament, and instead of just verbally providing me directions, she personally walked me to the church steps.

"I take you dere," she insisted.

You could count on the ates and kuyas to get you out of difficult situations too. Once while trying to do some sightseeing, a peal of thunder and large raindrops drove me and three other volunteers into the old, dimly lit gatehouse of the thousand-year-old Intramuros heritage site. What had begun as a nice, casual stroll around Manila's historical area turned into four naive volunteers trapped in a dark gatehouse with no option but to watch the rain gather in the streets outside. The downpour formed a swirling river of floodwater in mere minutes. I laughed as some local street kids splashed around stark-naked without a care in the world. While everyone else had run for cover, gripping umbrellas and hailing taxis, the boys enjoyed themselves as they swam and played, laughing and screaming in delight.

As I stood watching them, the flood made its way into the gatehouse, slowly, without alarm. "We'll just wait it out and leave when it stops raining so hard," I reasoned to my friends. They agreed.

Ten minutes later our waiting-it-out idea began to falter. The water level inside the gatehouse was no longer laughable. We stood near the walls on two-foot ledges; it wouldn't be long before the water would reach us. The thought of wading through all that water to get outside was less than appealing. That was when a kuya outside noticed our predicament and signaled to us if we required his services.

"Kuya! Kuya! Come help us!" we yelled.

Riding a pedal-powered rickshaw with a plastic-covered seating area, the kuya came down into the gatehouse to rescue us.

"Twenty pesos per person," he said.

We looked at each other then looked at the imminent rising water. Twenty pesos it was.

Giggling at the ridiculousness of the situation, we tried loading all four of us into the rickshaw. It was an awkward endeavor, which resulted in soggy shoes and pant legs. So much for the trying-to-stay-dry plan. The kuya drove us outside into the street where we transferred to a waiting taxi. We burst out laughing as we tumbled into the backseat and shoved eighty pesos at the kuya for his "rescue." He had driven us a mere twenty feet. "That was the best twenty pesos I've ever spent!"

~~~

Almost every year for Thanksgiving, I traveled to Sagada to meet up with other volunteers for our special Thanksgiving dinner tradition. Most American holidays spent in the Philippines were filled with strange emotions. You start off sad because you miss your family. You feel nostalgic and depressed that you won't be doing the same traditions you've done since you were little. And you get strangely patriotic about random things like turkeys, cranberry sauce, and pumpkin pie. I spent my first Thanksgiving in the Philippines at a pizza parlor with a few volunteer friends. Although it was nice to be with other Americans, I was disappointed not to have a real Thanksgiving feast. That's why, after that year, I always looked forward to the Sagada gathering.

I remember how fun it was for my first Sagada Thanksgiving experience. First, several volunteers took charge of the large fire pit at our hostel, and then the food preparations consumed us for the remainder of the day. I helped prepare stuffing and then chopped apples for the apple turnovers. By dinnertime, we gathered in the large dining room of the hostel, which overlooked a gorgeous view of rice terraces set against a mountain backdrop. The Sagada wind blew over the houses and brought with it a whiff of pine needles and fresh air. Even more gorgeous than the view was the display of food set out on one long table. It was one of the best Thanksgiving feasts I'd ever experienced—no Peace Corps goggles involved.

A few days after the much-needed American Thanksgiving party, I set off with several volunteers for a trip we had planned to see the Banaue Rice Terraces in the mountain province of Ifugao. The terraces are a UNESCO World Heritage Site, and some refer to them as the unofficial Eighth Wonder of the World. When we reached Banaue, we hired a local Filipino guide to take us to Batad, a village several kilometers away that was notoriously hard to reach.

In the open-air jeepney, the wind gushed through my hair and set my spirits high as we rumbled through villages past rivers, rice terraces, and houses jutting off the sides of cliffs. Children playing outside their homes stared up at us as we flew by. The mountain slopes, covered in greenery, reflected the morning rays of sun and beckoned us further in and higher up. After an hour, we slowed down. At the very end of the dirt road, resting halfway off the cliff edge was a small store stocked with supplies—snack food, water bottles, coconut water, souvenirs—and adjacent was the trailhead to Batad. Our guide instructed us to buy water. Lots of it.

There were no drivable roads that led to Batad. The only way to get there was to hike down into the village. In fact, the only way villagers had access to outside supplies was either by carrying it themselves or by hiring porters to jog down the mountain path balancing a pole with baskets tied on either end stuffed full of various goods. Soda cans, beer bottles, laundry soap, coffee—all nestled inside, weight balanced craftily. These men could reach the village in around twenty minutes. For everyone else (basically us foreigners), it took an hour or more to reach the village.

"Kuya, is the hike hard?" I asked our guide. He shook his head no.

Our long-haired guide was dressed in shorts, a dirty red shirt, and flip-flops. He also carried a tiny backpack with water. *Flip-flops, eh? It must not be a very difficult journey to Batad.*

Next to the roadside store, I saw a giant stack of sticks with a sign that read "Walking sticks for rent." I scoffed at the idea. *Hah! Walking sticks are for wimps.* I laughed to myself as I observed other tourists selecting ones from the pile. *If Kuya Flip-Flops doesn't need a walking stick, then I don't need one either.*

"Let's go," Kuya Flip-Flops said as he turned to lead our group down the path to Batad. An hour and a half later, we entered Batad with legs shaking and sweat slipping off our bodies.

"Let's take picture," Kuya Flip-Flops suggested at a special lookout. My "moisture wicking" T-shirt was soaked through. The afternoon sun blinded me, and I squinted with a scowl at the camera. I had no interest in viewpoints or cameras at that moment.

"OK, you eat first and then we hike," Kuya Flip-Flops told our group.

"Yes! Food!" I cried out as we collapsed on benches at the weathered wood table of our guest house. I scarfed a mound of adobo and rice until I felt more energized. Then, slipping on some hiking shoes and grabbing a water bottle, I joined our group outside. Kuya Flip-Flops nodded and we followed, crossing large water-filled terraces, treading carefully along the handcrafted stone walls.

"You see all dese rice terraces here? Da families each have der own terraces dat dey plant and harvest." Kuya Flip-Flops gestured to the giant terraces surrounding us.

I looked at the amphitheater, a large bowl of stacked rice terraces rising upward. *All of this is farmed by hand? Incredible.*

"Even after da end of harvest," Kuya Flip-Flops continued, "da rice produced is still not enough to feed all da people in da village. Many families also buy commercial rice from nearby towns. Dey also work in da big towns when it not rice season so dey have enough money."

*Not enough rice?* I looked across the vast expanse of terraces. The villagers labored months to harvest their rice, and it was still not enough. It was baffling to me.

Kuya Flip-Flops navigated the way as we skirted through the terraces and over the next hill. The scent of fresh, overturned dirt and warm grass filled the afternoon mixed with the smell of my sweat. As we climbed down the steep edge of the hillside, I flattered myself in thinking that it wasn't too strenuous.

At the bottom of the cliffs, we reached Tappiya Falls. The water was a dark forest green, highlighted by the afternoon streams of sunlight. Rocks edged the pool and spread outward forming a gray beach of smooth, rounded stones and pebbles. Tall stacks of these rocks jutted upward, one on top of another, balancing precariously like circular Jenga towers. The waterfall crashed down in one thick column creating a dull roar. The only other sounds I could hear were the footsteps and laughter we made as we tried to take silly pictures against the waterfall backdrop.

After a tranquil and languid hour spent at the falls, grueling work lay ahead as we returned back along the trail. Steep steps, where there even were steps, loomed above us on the path. The places where there was only dirt or gravel made for a slippery incline, but we clamored upward. The sun slipped behind the mountains, urging our hike onward in order to beat the fading daylight. The air had cooled off, but sweat was dripping steadily from my entire body. I began to regret my disdainful attitude about renting walking sticks. Alas, our beloved kuya, wearing nothing but flimsy flip-flops, hadn't even broken a sweat.

"Did you have a good time?" Kuya Flip-Flops asked when we reached the guest house. "You go eat your dinner now, hah."

"Yes! Food!" I cried out and finished off another plate of rice and meat. After dinner, laden with exhaustion, I fell asleep as soon as I lay down in my room at the hostel.

Before I even opened my eyes in the morning, I could feel the soreness in my muscles. *Hay naku! What a hike!* Sitting up, I pulled aside the faded lace curtain that hung over the open window. Right outside was a view of the entire amphitheater of rice terraces, the still water reflecting the mountain landscape on the opposite side of the valley. Only an occasional rooster in the distance disturbed the peaceful silence of the village. I pondered on how this place was so out of the way that not many people would get to enjoy this remarkable view. I savored it a few extra minutes so that I would remember how everything looked. Photographs could never do justice to a scene like this.

As we hoisted our packs once again, our group set out for the trail leading back to the main road. The shadows in rich green and blue fell into the deep crevices of the terrain. Along the trail, crooked and windblown trees with papery white bark stretched toward a cloudless blue sky. Kuya Flip-Flops stood waiting at the top of the hill a short distance ahead. Still wearing his worn flip-flops, he looked back and smiled at us. A light breeze whispered past, bringing with it the fragrance of Cordillera mountain air.

At the trailhead entrance, our jeepney stood waiting to take us back to Banaue. When we finally reached the center of town, we said our goodbyes to Kuya Flip-Flops.

"Thank you, kuya," I said to him.

"Take care," he said as he smiled again and waved goodbye. Kuya Flip-Flops and the stories he told of his community over the past few days had solidified my understanding of Cordilleran folk. The way they lived their lives was impressive to me. Whether they worked in the fields, managed the chores of the home, or ran their own business, I was always in awe of the strength they portrayed. Not just physical but also mental, emotional, and spiritual strength. Mountain life was hard for those who didn't have a steady source of income. It didn't take much to convince me that the mountain residents in the Cordilleran region must have been born with superpowers. When I reflected on it more, I had seen these same key traits of strength and perseverance in the ates and kuyas all over the Philippines. In fact, they conveyed many other admirable characteristics—generosity, hospitality, friendliness, kindness, community support—and I could see how those traits weaved together to form what I saw as the spirit of the Philippines, or the Filipino way.

In the sleepy town of Banaue, I spent a few hours lounging around waiting to board the night bus that would bring me back to Baguio. I wandered through dimly lit souvenir shops with thick layers of dust covering the shelves and perused the assortment of local products—jewelry, handwoven purses, carved wooden Igorot statues, and Ifugao province coffee. I was struck by the vibrantly colored patterns of the traditional mountain weavings, similar to what they had in Sagada and Baguio. Stacks of handwoven material in bright red, green, blue, and yellow had always proved to be a feast for my eyes. They were a unique product of the mountain provinces and emitted the beauty of native mountain culture.

Late that afternoon, seated in a cozy café with a few other volunteers, I drank Ifugao roasted coffee and dove into one of my books. Refreshing mountain wind blew through the window, and I lost myself in a daydream amidst the terraced town of Banaue.

Mountain roads. Colorful weavings. Coffee. The ates and kuyas. The Filipino way. Each region and its people were marked by random pieces of everyday life, forming themselves into a more solid picture of what I had come to know as the Philippines.

## 25

## IT'S DA WEATHER

By the time I had settled into life abroad, I thought I had it all figured out. I was Miss Filipino Culture Queen and resident expert on living in the Philippines. "That's what you think about Filipino culture? No, that's not right. Let me tell you how it *really* is." I was living the life, and I had the nicknames to prove it.

"Hello, Ate Debs."

"Good morning, Madame Devora."

"Hi, Ate Bevs."

"Mestiza!"

"Hello, Teacher!"

Everyone knew my name, where I came from, where I was going, what I'd bought, and how much my rent cost each month. Cultural norms I swore I'd never accept had now become part of my everyday life. Sometimes it *was* nice to have someone to lean against in the crowded jeepney after a long day at work. And who doesn't want to videoke at nine in the morning?

"You're so Filipino," my friend teased when I took out my umbrella to shield myself from the hot sun.

"I know."

"You're so Filipino," I was told when I confessed that I was making garlic rice for dinner.

"Yeah, I know."

"We were supposed to meet an hour ago."

"I'm on Filipino time."

I spouted my "where are you going?" and "where did you come from?" greetings like nobody's business. I stared unapologetically at people as they walked down the street. I reveled in tambay time. I raised my eyebrows to answer yes. I pointed with my lips. And I liked it. As I grew more confident and proud of my accomplishments in "cultural integration," I thought the world was mine. I forgot where I was.

One morning, after my usual coffee, I headed off into town for a haircut. I'd experienced my fair share of bad haircuts in the Philippines, so this time I decided to try a salon owned by an acquaintance of mine. I figured I might be better off going there where I could at least explain how I envisioned my ideal haircut. When I arrived at her studio, she was nowhere to be found. A middle-aged woman motioned for me to take a seat. I felt a bit uneasy that my friend was not around, but I sat down anyway. Aside from the several women lounging around gossiping, I was the only client there. On top of that, the stylist didn't speak English very well and wasn't catching my vision for how I wanted my hair cut.

Speaking clearly in English so she would understand, I told her to just trim it about an inch and make sure it was layered. "Layers, Ate. Layers," I emphasized. I watched her in the mirror to make sure she wasn't doing anything weird.

Snip-snip. Little locks of hair fell to the floor. I didn't notice anything out of the ordinary, so I let her continue. Snip-snip, cut-cut. Then I turned my head slightly and noticed something was off. "Stop," I cried out. "No, Ate, not like that!"

She got flustered and started pulling out magazines, and we both flipped through the pages trying to find an example of the haircut I was hoping for. The problem became glaringly obvious after looking through the Filipino beauty magazines—Filipina-style haircuts were much different from American haircuts. She was trying to cut my hair the way a typical Filipina would like to have it. That meant rounded, thick, and fluffy instead of the thinned-out layered ends I was hoping for.

I couldn't find a single picture that matched the style I wanted. The other women in the room, roused out of their boredom by my predicament, began trying to help me and my stylist. One woman pointed at a picture of a Filipina with long, curly locks.

"You mean like dis? Only with straight hair?" she asked.

"But it's curly," I shot back. "How am I supposed to know what it looks like when it's straight?" I rolled my eyes. "Never mind," I finally grumbled. "Just finish the other side, and leave it at that."

The stylist did her best to finish the haircut, and I did my best to smile, pay, and leave. I went home, looked at my hair in the mirror, and cried. One side was two inches longer than the other. I felt like a major component of my dignity had been swept up and dumped in the trash along with my chopped off hair. All I could see was months of ponytails until my hair grew out and I could get it done the right way, back in America.

I tried to convince myself that maybe it had just been a long week. Maybe I just needed some chocolate and a bottle of rice wine. Unfortunately, I had neither. The only thing left to do was to wallow in my own misery, play sad and depressing songs on repeat, and stare at the ceiling.

I knew I was being overdramatic, but I couldn't help it. A volunteer's service is often marked by the signature roller coaster highs and lows. My mistake was not that I had gone to that particular salon but that I had become so self-assured of my cross-cultural abilities. I thought I'd become immune to the emotional roller coaster. I thought I was past feeling like one day was amazing and the next was a complete disaster. It used to be that even the smallest of annoyances could bring me crashing down. I remember when the Peace Corps officials showed us newbies a chart forewarning when volunteers typically started to feel depressed and when they would start to feel more positive. When things were going well at work or you made a new friend, you were on a high. When your health plummeted or you got annoyed at people staring at you because you were American, you descended into the lows.

In fact, during my first few months in Baguio, I had started on a high, reveling in the excitement of a new city and a volunteer job. But it wasn't long before I found myself down in a low period. Part of it had been difficult cultural adjustments and frustration at work, but a lot of it had to do with a cold I had developed. My health took a hit when I developed a mysterious cough that lasted for weeks on end.

"It's da weather," parents at the school would state matter-of-factly in explanation of why I had gotten sick.

"Oh yes, it's da weather. First it's hot, den it's really cold. It's da weather," another parent remarked to me about my cough. *Or maybe it's the fact that I work with kids all day. Or maybe it's because I have mold in my house!*

"You're sick again, Ate Debs? Why?" Carmelita would ask. She never got sick.

"I...do-don't...know-ho," I coughed out.

"That cough sounds really bad, Ate. It must be da weather."

"No, it's no-not the wea-heather," I hacked from the depths of my lungs.

If I wasn't sick and hacking out my lungs, my stomach would most likely be having issues. Some of the strange foods I ate did not always agree with me. Crying out in pain in my CR was an inevitable part of my life.

"It's dat weather again, Ate."

*No, it is not the weather!*

After such a prolonged sickness, it was understandable why I experienced such a low moment in my service. An unhealthy body resulted in an unhealthy emotional and mental state of mind as well. Eventually my body adjusted to the environment and conditions in Baguio, and I hadn't gotten that sick in a long time. Even so, during the months that followed, if it wasn't my health that took me down, it was my insecurities. Things I hear regularly in the Philippines:

> "Teacher, you look fat today."
> "What happened to your face? Is dat a pimple?"
> "Teacher, you have a baby," students say as they grab my stomach. (*I really need to stop eating so much pandesal.*)
> "Ha, ha. You talk punny, Teacher."
> "You are past da prime age for marriage."
> "Hey, half-half!"

Living in the Philippines was one endless roller coaster. *Why couldn't the Philippines just be more like America?* I vented one day. Bad haircuts, rude comments, over-inquisitive ates, being hit on by every single taxi driver, being told "it's da weather" as an explanation for everything, still being forced to eat food I disliked. *Enough!*

*Who are you to judge the Philippines? I thought you were Miss Filipino Culture Queen?* My practical self tried to intervene with my complaining self. But in that moment, I refused to listen to my practical self. Instead, I indulged my complaining self. After all, I struggled living alone, being far away from American family and friends, feeling less and less a part of their lives as they continued to live without me around. Right now, they were back home enjoying luxurious comfort—driving cars, taking hot showers, getting nice haircuts—and I was alone wondering if I had made the right decision. *Did I even belong here?* There were moments in every day that made me feel like I was a failure. People laughed at my accent or my inability to master the language. People commented on me gaining weight, or that I had pimples on my face.

Whether or not I plunged into a low always hinged on the little things. The seemingly insignificant things were ultimately what exposed the loopholes of my pride and fleeting feelings of cultural belonging. My life in the Philippines felt like a constant battle between wanting to love every moment and the temptation to throw up my hands in exasperation at a culture I couldn't quite figure out.

I was fraying at the edges, just like my favorite pair of jeans after countless uses, handwashing, and wringing had taken its toll. I longed to go home. I missed America. I had never been the type of volunteer who kept track of how many days I had left, counting them down one by one until my service contract ended. But if I was honest with myself, there were times when I looked at the calendar with wistful longing.

One evening after a particularly bad day, I was in the jeepney on my ride home from the market when the tears just started coming. I couldn't stop them if I tried. Because we were packed so closely together, I couldn't move my arms very far to wipe the tears away, so I just let them fall, trying to avoid the curious gaze of the mother sitting across from me. I put my head down, chin resting on my bag. A resignation of tiredness. In fact, everyone on that jeep looked tired. It must have been a long day for all.

*I wish I was in America,* I sighed.

I had the option to leave. It's something every Peace Corps volunteer has in the back of their mind. Although we sign up for a two-year contract, if at any time we decide to leave, we can. I could escape from this world that was not my own, to turn away from what I'd seen and encountered. I had an out if I wanted it. But somehow, I kept going. I was determined to keep going.

And then, just over two years into my service, I had an incident that sent me straight into the deepest of lows.

## 26

## WHO IS YOUR KASAMA?

"Get on a bus to Manila." Those were my doctor's words. The state of my asthma—generally mild and under control—had become an increasing concern in the last few weeks, and tonight I was having trouble sleeping because I couldn't breathe. So at two o'clock in the morning, I found myself on a bus headed down the mountain, lightheaded and struggling for breath. Outside my window I watched the lights of Baguio disappear slowly into patches of fog as we descended the mountain. Then regret settled in. *How was I going to survive the next six hours to Manila in my current condition?* I must not have emphasized to my doctor the extent of my symptoms. Why else would he have told me to embark on a six-hour bus ride when I clearly needed immediate attention? *This is a mistake.*

By three o'clock in the morning, I had abandoned the idea of reaching Manila and instead had boarded a different bus returning to Baguio. By the time I reached Baguio's city center, caught a taxi to the nearest hospital and walked into the ER, I was exhausted and anxious for what was to come. The last thing I needed was to be greeted with one more reminder of how alone I felt.

"Who is your *kasama*?" the ER nurse asked me as I sat waiting on the squeaky teal plastic mattress. *Who is your kasama?* It was a question I had become very familiar with since moving to the Philippines. A kasama was a friend, a companion. Filipinos hardly ever went somewhere without a kasama—it was just part of the culture. I, however, lived by myself in a one-bedroom house. I had just returned from my attempted bus-ride-to-Manila fiasco, and it was already early morning. *Of course I didn't have a kasama!* I scowled to myself as the nurse put a plastic mask over my nose and mouth and made me breath in some vapor medication for a few minutes. She then informed me that I had experienced a severe asthma attack. I was in shock. It was the first time I had experienced one as an adult, and I hadn't recognized the signs.

"Who is your kasama?" another nurse asked me as she wheeled me in a chair to my hospital room.

"I don't have one."

"None? Why?!" She could not fathom my lack of kasama.

"Who is your kasama?" the x-ray attendants asked curiously as they pushed me into the correct positions for front, side, and back views.

"It's just me."

"Oooh, she's an English speaker!" They chattered to each other with excited, nervous tones. This was typical behavior. Medical office interns never liked to be the one to assist the patient who spoke English.

"OK...um...excuse me, ma'am," one woman ventured. "Would you please hab a seat right dere? Dank you. We will...um...hab the, *anong tawag?* Hay naku!" she exclaimed amid laughter from her peers.

"Nosebleed!" they teased her and giggled. They held fingers up to their noses to emphasize the joke. "Nosebleed! Ha, ha!"

"Nosebleed. Ha, ha," I joined in with less than enthusiastic chuckling. I wasn't in the mood for jokes in that moment.

Back in my hospital room, another nurse took my vitals and then asked if I had a kasama. There was a small cot in my room left specifically for the purpose of letting a kasama sleep there overnight. "I live by myself," I told her. What else was I supposed to say? I had contacted my friends and host family already, and they were planning to stop by later that day to visit me. Why did I need a constant companion by my side every single second of the day?

The nurse left the room and I couldn't help but notice how lonely the space felt when it was just me. This was the first time I had ever been admitted to an emergency room and a hospital stay. *It's just my luck,* I sighed to myself. My first time *would* be in the Philippines where my Filipino language abilities were less than par. I pulled up the covers around me and stared at the empty kasama cot.

This isn't what I had envisioned when I first learned I would be living in the Philippines. Two years ago I had embraced my assignment to the Philippines with open arms. *This was my dream. I made this happen.* I had rejoiced in the prospect of living in the country of my dad's birth and immersing in a culture I had always longed to know. But those thoughts were now the furthest thing from my mind as I lay alone and exhausted on the cold hospital bed. I waved my cell phone in the air trying to get a strong enough signal to contact my family in America. I sent out a few texts letting them know what had happened. Just thinking about my family and how worried they might be made me well up inside. Even as I texted to my mom, "I'm doing OK," I started to cry. *I'm not totally OK.*

I cried until I became drowsy from exhaustion. Then I curled my knees up against my chest and pulled the thin white sheet around me. I had never felt so far from home. Maybe having a kasama with me wouldn't have been so bad after all.

## 27

# ALLERGIC

I checked out of the hospital a few days later with several bags of prescriptions in tow. Over the next few weeks, my main goal was to get my asthma under control. In doing so, I was disconcerted by what I observed. It became obvious that the prescriptions doing the most to improve my health were allergy medications. I'm sure there was a perfectly reasonable medical explanation for this, but the only thing that ran through my mind was something more illogical: I had become allergic to the Philippines. *Really, Philippines?* All these months of trying to integrate, to be accepted, to learn about my Filipino roots, and here I was, allergic to the Philippines.

The irony of this realization felt like the final blow. I was defeated. The Philippines had beaten me down and tested me in many ways before—insidious mold, persistent questions, unapologetic stares, dreary rainstorms—but I always kept going. From day one, I was determined to survive it all. I'd even willingly signed up for a third year of service. I was committed. But now it felt like the Philippines and everything it entails had finally taken a toll on my overall physical and mental health. Had I met my match?

I thought about my own lola who retired in the Philippines. After living in Guam for many years, she had finally been able to return to her homeland. But even she was plagued by her asthma and eventually was forced to leave because her health was in such jeopardy. Was this my time as well?

Throughout my internal battles wrestling with doubt and purpose, a small part of me understood that the health issues, bad haircuts, lousy weather, annoying cultural mannerisms, and other surface-level things were not the true sources of my frustration and anger. They only symbolized the distress and discomfort of behaviors and situations that I didn't fully understand or accept. I wasn't allergic to the Philippines; I was just resistant and broken-down.

While I *was* physically sick—feeling discouraged, inadequate, weak—it only mirrored the strong sense of inadequacy and inability I felt in confronting the poverty and injustice I'd witnessed. I had watched whole communities of families suffer and knew the unfairness of the situation they were born into. I had witnessed those who chose the easy way out of their situation through lying, stealing, and cheating. I had seen and felt the discouragement of honest individuals and families who hoped for a better life without ever seeing much, if any, improvement. These experiences made me angry, but mostly I felt frustrated that I was unable to do much to make it better.

Sometimes in the Philippines it felt like there was no escape from an overwhelming sense of helplessness. Helpless in fending off life's problems, helpless at alleviating any of the pain. I joined the Peace Corps because I felt called to help others, to make a difference in the world. Making a difference was something I strived for daily. But I had learned over the past few years in the Philippines that making a difference didn't happen in the way I had originally expected. It definitely did not come through large feats or acts. It was usually the small and sometimes seemingly insignificant things that made the most impact in people's day-to-day lives.

I recalled the year before on a rainy Saturday afternoon when there had been nothing to do except play guitar to the empty streets and watch the rain pour down. I had felt discouraged and was questioning whether I was really making any sort of difference. Rain splattered on the cement road, a rhythmic, soothing sound. I sat outside my house jamming on my guitar with David and his friend Rafael. Music intertwined with the pitter-patter of droplets.

"So, why did you come here, anyway? Why did you decide to be a volunteer?" David asked during a lull in our jamming. He lit up a two-peso cigarette and inhaled a few puffs, waiting for my answer. I launched into my make-a-difference-in-the-world spiel.

"So, you don't get a salary?" he asked.

"No. It's volunteer service." Rain pelted down harder, but we sat unmoving, listening to the sounds of the storm.

"And you want to change the world?"

"Yeah."

"You aren't going to change the world, you know."

Patter-patter, drip-drip.

"I know." Changing the world was more of a cliché anyway. I wasn't out to change the world by myself. "I didn't expect to," I clarified. "I guess I'm just a seed planter." The rumble of the rain rose. It slapped the leaves of the pomelo tree; it bounced off the banana palms. The metal roofs of the little cement houses clamored with rhythmic drumming.

"Even if it's a little, it still makes a difference," Rafael chimed in. I looked at him in surprise. He was normally too shy to say much in English.

"Yeah, Rafael, even if it's a little," I responded. We resumed playing. The songs were almost mute against the beating of the rain. A quick breath of wind sent a spray toward us. Gentle, yet powerful; exhilarating, yet mysterious. Philippine rain caused sorrow, destruction, and disarray without regret. It could beat anything into the mud, into nothingness. But, Philippine rain also gave energy. It gave vigor and life. It brought joy. There were always two ways to understand Philippine rain.

*Even if it's just a little.*

I came to the conclusion that my small ways of helping *were* meaningful, they were making a difference, even if not on a large scale, and I was OK with that. Truly, the most ironic part was that this whole experience had made a huge difference in *my* life, as if I had received more than I was able to give. In fact, as glamorous as my service abroad seemed to those on the outside, it wasn't the fact that I was trying to make a difference that had kept me going through the lows of my time there. It was something more. Living in the Philippines as a Filipino American had changed the stakes. It forced me to encounter this experience on a more personal level. *What would my life look like if I had been born in the Philippines? How would I be different than I am now?*

As I faced the Philippines head on and grappled with these questions, I knew now that besides gaining a deeper understanding of the culture, the way of life, and that distinct Filipino way, I wanted to know what that meant for the millions of families living in poverty there. Ultimately, I wanted to live out the deep sense of solidarity I felt with the Philippines. But those words were tricky. I often found myself avoiding the very things I said I wanted to embrace, whether out of resistance, fear, or simply longing to be somewhere familiar and comfortable. I would push these things away using excuses like being allergic to the Philippines or that I was tired of getting annoying comments about my physical appearance. I was good at building up walls.

Sometimes my attempts at solidarity were laughable. Could I really claim solidarity with the people of the Philippines simply because I'd screamed at bugs in my room, wasn't able to buy my favorite brand-name pair of shoes, and couldn't drink Starbucks for six months? I often bore my challenges of living with the bare necessities with a sense of pride. I took bucket baths with water that had been heated over my stove. I rode a jeepney twenty minutes into town every few days to buy food from the market because I didn't own a refrigerator. I didn't have a TV, much less a couch. I washed my clothes in a plastic pail, wrung them out, and hung them up on a line to dry. I thought I was badass for "going without." However, I couldn't escape the fact that in a few months I'd return back to the US to my former life, a life where I'd never again have to hand-wash my clothes or kill giant bugs on the wall. I had no way of knowing what it was truly like for someone to have to live in those conditions for their entire life. I was not born into it, and as a volunteer, I had the option to leave at any point. Most of the people I encountered on a daily basis did not have that luxury. They were stuck in the life they'd been born into.

One afternoon while lounging in my house, I glanced out the window and saw Jayden's mom collecting laundry from their clothesline. She did this almost every single day. *Now there's a strong woman.* She washed the clothes for a family of ten, cooked their meals three times a day, attended to all the children, cleaned the entire house, and managed the family store. I looked at my own kitchen, dirty dishes in the sink. I remembered the pile of clothes in my room I'd been meaning to get around to for the past three weeks. I complained about my life because I'd get to leave it one day; she didn't complain because it was what she'd be doing for the rest of her life.

Her example solidified for me the Filipino traits I'd been so drawn to and in awe of since coming to the country. Strength.

Perseverance. I started recalling all the people in my community who demonstrated these qualities. Ma'am Ligaya once told me that she worked to pay for her own schooling when she was younger. She moved to Baguio City from a mountain province at a young age and began working as a maid.

"In the province, my skin peeled off like flakes because I didn't have any nutrition," she told me. "We could not afford to eat meat or vegetables. We ate rice mixed with seasoning or sauce. Maybe soy sauce with *sili*, like this," she pointed toward our lunch plates on the table.

Every day my co-worker Rita, a new Australian volunteer, and I mixed a tiny dab of potent spicy chili sauce called sili into our rice. One day, we decided to have a sili challenge where we had to mix an entire spoonful of it into our rice and eat the entire thing. Ma'am Ligaya reluctantly agreed to join our "fun" event.

"Ready?" Rita asked.

"Game!" I yelled. Rita and I spooned mouthfuls of rice and chased them down with gulps of water. Ma'am Ligaya, on the other hand, was slow and steady. She almost cried from the potent spice, but she made it to the end. We cheered each other on, and then the game ended with uproarious laughter. With Ma'am Ligaya it was always laughter, always a ready smile. In fact, what struck me the most about the people I encountered in the Philippines was their incredible resiliency and ability to persevere through anything with a smile. *Filipino perseverance.* I needed some Filipino perseverance right about now.

~~~

A few weeks later, Jayden and I sat at the kitchen table talking and listening to music. Our conversation rolled around from school and family to sharing our favorite new songs on the radio. And then I came up with an interesting question for him.

"So Jayden, if you had three wishes, what would you wish for?"

"I wish for all the people of the world to be safe and protected," he said thoughtfully.

"Oh, well, that's very nice. What's your second wish?"

"That there will be no more poor people in the world."

"Yes, that is definitely a good wish. And your last wish?"

"That nothing bad will happen to people. Like typhoons and robbers and like that."

*Who is this kid?* I was in awe. I didn't know too many eleven-year-old kids who used up their free wishes on world peace instead of toys and candy. But Jayden did. Jayden, with his oversized and over-stretched T-shirts, had a way of touching your heart when you least expected it. His unintentionally profound words latched on to me, reminding me of the joy and hope I had experienced in the Philippines through the many relationships I had formed.

My neighbors, friends, and students modeled to me the tenacity of those struggling to find a way to a better life, and it challenged me to question my own ability to persevere. But I was inspired by the generosity of those who had nothing more to give than smiles, laughter, and joy, and yet they gave it all willingly, even to me as a stranger. The pride of their tradition, heritage, and culture spilled out in their hospitality and that distinct Filipino way.

I could choose to view my life in the Philippines through the lens of months of bucket baths, electricity brownouts, monsoon floods, mosquito nets, and packed-to-the-brim buses. Or I could choose to focus on the smiling faces of my students, the cheery greetings as I walked down the street, the toothless grin of the jeepney kuya, the example of perseverance, and the sound of heavy raindrops infusing the farmlands and vegetable terraces with growth and life.

There were always two ways to understand Philippine rain, and there were always two ways to view Philippine life. It was tempting and easy to focus only on the annoying or negative aspects. I could vent about how frustrating life could be and how strange Filipinos acted sometimes. Or I could take the time to look deeper and be amazed by Filipinos whose beauty could only come from their strength, endurance, and hope. I could choose to look at the positive characteristics of the culture, how Filipinos are some of the most hospitable, generous, and friendly people on the planet.

But my deepest realization didn't stop there. It took courage for me to go one step further. I had to look at the Philippines as a whole. My truest understanding of the country came when I accepted the rich complexity of the culture with both the positive and negative aspects existing in one cohesive entity. I had to acknowledge there were things about the culture that I didn't like and would never understand, but that didn't mean I couldn't feel like I was a part of the Philippines or that I didn't belong. It also didn't negate my desire to be in solidarity with my community.

My path was undeniably different than those I came to know and love in the Philippines. After all, I was not born there. But I had a burning desire to gain the deepest understanding of my heritage that I could. I had witnessed Philippine life for the past few years, and that counted for much more than I gave myself credit for. And more than anything, I genuinely cared about living in solidarity. I had a deep desire to learn the stories of what others experienced, to be present with them in their joy and their pain, and to take whatever action I could to alleviate their suffering.

I felt like I finally started to grasp the meaning of the word solidarity when I removed my Peace Corps goggles, took the time to understand the intricacies and realities of the country as a whole, and was present with my friends, neighbors, and students through the ups and downs of their daily lives. I finally understood what it meant to be Filipino more than I ever had. I was connecting. Moving forward, I knew there was always more than one way of looking at Philippine rain.

Solidarity. Wishes. Poverty. Perseverance. Rain. Resilience. Laughter. Smiles. That distinct Filipino way. My journey was not yet finished. America could wait.

## 28

# TEACH ME SOMETHING DIFFICULT

Every now and then my music students would have little outbursts stemming from the positive emotions that come from having learned or completed something complicated. Once, Kenneth ran home from Guitar Club yelling spontaneously, "I LOVE SOLOING!" It was a happy outburst paired with a wild-eyed face of exhilaration. I couldn't help but laugh with delight.

My favorite outburst was during one of the music café nights. The Jazz Rockers performed a few numbers that really wowed the audience, so afterward I treated the band members to some hot chocolate and desserts. It was an attempt to reward them for enduring my endless practices. As Mikky energetically munched on the sugary snacks he clutched in each fist, he ventured to tell me something in English. He was grinning, illuminated by the sort of glow derived from having just completed an amazing performance.

"Teacher, you get da prize!"

"Oh, really?! What prize?"

"Teacher, you get da prize for cooling!"

"Oh…umm, you mean being cool?"

"Yes, Teacher! You get da prize for being cool!"

Then there was another outburst just before Christmas when I took some of my music students to go caroling in the neighborhood. In the Philippines, children traditionally go caroling on the evenings preceding Christmas and receive pocket change in return from each house where they sing. Several of the kids caroling that night were in my jazz band and we brought a few guitars and beatboxes along. For a recent school Christmas event the band had performed "Winter Wonderland" and I decided to have them play it as we went caroling merrily through the neighborhood, performing the song at least once per house. At least once. Sometimes it was twice. It was the only Christmas song they had memorized.

I had also printed out song sheets for some easy Christmas carols and the corresponding chords, but since there were a lot of us, we always had to huddle together. The kids fumbled through the chords, not to mention the English lyrics for the more traditional songs, but at least "Winter Wonderland" was always perfect.

We began to stop at the homes of families we knew from the school. I recognized the path where we headed next, and as we approached the building, Sebastian told us it was his house.

"Sebastian," I nudged him. "I didn't realize this was your house. I've been here before. A long time ago, when I first arrived in Baguio." I still remember how his baby brother grabbed at the peanut butter jar as his mom chatted with us about her life.

"Yes, Teacher, I remember that. Yes, this is my house," he replied bashfully. His mother stood in the entryway, also smiling bashfully as our choir serenaded her with "Winter Wonderland."

By the end of the evening, after splitting up their earnings, the students went home amazed and grateful at the pile of coins they each grasped in their hands.

"Teacher, can we do dis every night?!" Jonas and Mikky blurted out. "Dis is fun!"

I smiled and shook my head while some of the other teachers laughed. "Good night, everyone. Take care!" I said as we all parted ways.

I walked home listening to distant voices drifting in the dark as other singing groups made their rounds throughout the neighborhood. Hundreds of stars scattered across the open sky, peeking out from behind the dark outline of houses, palm trees, and my beloved mountains upon mountains.

~~~

Over the years, I watched many of my students grow up and transform. Samuel, Jun Jun, Benji, Esteban, and now even Jonas had entered high school—they were the "big kids" now, and it was time to put their skills to use. I began to energetically plan for a big arts camp during the summer.

"You'll be my guitar teachers at camp, yeah?" I asked Jun Jun, Benji, and Team English.

"OK, Teacher! Just show us what will we do," Jun Jun said. They were sitting around the office jamming on guitars when Kenneth and Josiah walked in.

"Hey, Kenneth, Josiah. Could you help me teach guitar at summer camp?" I asked them.

"OK, teacher," Kenneth agreed. "But you'll teach us difficult things too?"

"Yes, of course, Kenneth."

"Yay!" Josiah cheered. "Can you teach us something now, Teacher?"

~~~

The first day of the arts camp arrived, and hordes of kids filled the classrooms for each workshop. The room at the very end of the hallway was designated as the music workshop.

"OK, listen to me now, hah," I overheard Samuel begin as he addressed the little campers. That group of third-grade kids could not sit still or pay attention.

"Listen, all of you," Jun Jun hollered above the noise trying to back Samuel up. "Dis is how to hold your guitar."

I smirked in the doorway of the classroom.

"Teacher Debs, teaching kids is hard," Jun Jun told me later. "Dey don't like to listen." *And now you know how it felt when I taught you, ha!* I laughed, but I was proud of my little teachers. They were growing up, learning how to give back. During that week at the arts camp, I sat back and watched my guitar teachers in action. Samuel demonstrated his soloing skills to the wonderment of the little ones. Jun Jun wowed them with songs he could play from the radio. Kenneth and Josiah played difficult things. Mikky showed everyone how to play a baseline. Life was golden.

It was through my students that I learned the most about myself and about Filipino culture. Small ways were best. I watched how my students came to school each day with smiling faces, despite the home conditions they lived in. I admired the manner in which they conducted themselves in the face of hardship, how they proved their willingness and determination to excel and succeed. I laughed with delight at the jokes they told me, the pop songs they blasted from their cell phones, and the rambunctious and infectious energy they brought.

All of my students' lives began to slowly impress on me, revealing a deeper sense of life and culture in the Philippines. They provided a human face to something I had at first tried to intellectualize. Understanding Filipino culture was not just about getting some knowledge I had missed out on as a child or experiencing something I had never been exposed to. It wasn't about something I had to gain or become an expert in. It was not even about earning acceptance. Ultimately, it was the invitation to share in another's life. It was a living concept—the outpouring of everyday interconnectedness and community. Culture was connection. My students unknowingly revealed that to me and invited me into it on a daily basis.

The last few months of my service were marked by the familiar routine of students and guitars. Sometimes they were current students, sometimes former ones. They all drifted in and out of my days instilling a firm sense of purpose and ownership of the life I had created. With each day, they reaffirmed my commitment to fulfill my contract and persevere until the end.

Sometimes it was Kenneth and Josiah's eagerness that reminded me of why I stayed. "Teacher, can you teach me something difficult?" Kenneth would usually ask during lunchtime.

"OK, I have a new solo for you," I'd tell him.

"Yes! Is it difficult, Teacher?"

"Yes, it's very difficult."

"Yay!"

"Teacher, me too!" Josiah would yell as he ran into my office, wiping his face free of rice crumbs.

"First, go wash your hands," I chided.

Other times it was Jonas who gave me my daily reminder. "Hello, Teacher Debs," he called out as he entered the office.

"Team English! Yo! What's up?" I reached out my hand to give him a high five. "How's high school?"

"It's good, Teacher."

"You're studying hard?"

"Yes, Teacher."

"You're still playing guitar?"

"Yes, Teacher. Look, I can play a new song." He selected a guitar next to my desk and demonstrated a new song he'd taught himself.

"Wow, you're so good! You'll play with me again at the next café, yeah?"

"OK, Teacher! Can we play 'Winter Wonderland'?"

"Well, that's a Christmas song. Maybe another."

And sometimes it was my newer students, like Gerald, who brought me joy and a renewed sense of direction.

"How is Gerald doing in guitar?" a teacher asked me one day.

"Fine," I replied. "He's learning very fast, and he's one of my best students at the moment."

"That's good! In class, he struggles sometimes to keep up with da class work and da pace of other students," she confided.

I suspected that Gerald also didn't have too many friends and was more often than not the subject of bullying or teasing. That made me all the more protective of him. One month, I invited all the new guitar students to perform at the music café. All of them were too scared to do it.

"No one will perform?" I asked the kids one afternoon. "Owen? You don't want to perform?"

"No, Teacher. I'm too scared," he replied.

"It's OK, you don't have to be scared. It will be fun."

"Teacher, I don't like," he resisted.

"John?" I asked, scanning the room.

"NO, TEACHER!"

"Fine. Gerald? Will you perform?"

"Umm…OK, Teacher. I will perform," he replied despite the fear that boggled his eyes. And he did. Wiping his overly moist palms on his jeans, he played his chords, albeit with shaking hands, strumming faithfully to the end.

"Very good, Gerald! Were you nervous?"

"No, Teacher, I wasn't nervous at all."

"Oh…really? Not even a little bit?"

"No, Teacher, not even a little."

Gerald played again at the café performance the next month. On that occasion, his mom attended. He was very proud of himself as he sat next to her, the two of them eating cookies and drinking hot chocolate. He wasn't nervous that time either he assured me, face still glistening with sweat.

## 29

# PHILIPPINES, WE NEED TO TALK

M y favorite part of the day was the afternoon when the bell
rang to dismiss school. After school meant Guitar Club—
a few hours' worth of animated students demanding my
attention, discordant melodies and rhythms, and a cadence of
high-spiritedness and laughter. Even with the buzz of energy,
the afternoon moved like fragrant drizzled honey, slowing down
life just enough to revel in that familiar routine. The toting of
instruments back and forth from storage to our meeting space.
Floppy guitar cases, sections of the fabric now ripped or
unraveling from constant use. Chord fingerings etched out in
chalk on the blackboard. Dog-eared guitar booklets pulled out
of backpacks. Curious, wandering five-year-olds watching from
the doorway. The echo of bad acoustics from the cement walls.
The pounding of rain on the roof during monsoon season. The
eager strum-strum-strum of little musicians.

"Like dis, Teacher?"

"Oh yes, you're doing a good job! Almost there."

I was regularly teaching Gerald, a boy named Ryder, and a
roomful of other energetic and rambunctious music students.
Kenneth and Josiah were still around, but they preferred
watching tutorial videos on my laptop in order to learn more

"difficult things." They didn't want to bother with the beginner guitar lessons.

"Teacher, Teacher, chords!" Gerald flapped his guitar book in the air at me. I tested him on the chords he had learned. He hadn't memorized all the ones I'd assigned yet, but I gave him a sticker for the "G" and "Am" chords.

"Teacher, Teacher, 'Ode to Joy'!" Owen called out. I sat on the yellow knee-high table next to him and assessed his ability to play the song correctly.

"*Halos na!* Almost there!" I told him. "*Malapit na!* So close!"

"Teacher, me now!"

"Teacher, chords again!"

"No, me first, Teacher Debs."

I craved the chaotic environment of Guitar Club where everyone was pulling for my attention all at the same time. I drifted from student to student offering advice and testing them on their songs. Each time they could successfully play a song, they'd get a sticker in their guitar workbook. I learned that stickers were a great motivator. I had started using them for fun in my summer guitar classes and witnessed their power to keep kids excited for learning more.

"If you can perfect your song, you'll get a sticker."

"STICKERS??? Oooh, me, me, Teacher. Me, now!"

I also acquired my first Guitar Club assistant, Camille, a fifth-grade girl with long eyelashes and a demure smile. She originally showed up to Guitar Club with the mistaken impression that it was piano lessons but decided to hang around during the meetings every day anyway.

"Would you be interested in learning guitar, Camille?"

"No, Teacher. I don't like," she told me. But she watched with fascination while the other students practiced. She listened intently when I taught various techniques to the others. She remained in the periphery but still ever present. One day I finally asked her to be my assistant. She could at least have a job to do instead of just hanging around watching other kids.

"Can you take attendance?" I asked, officially assigning her a task. And then I forgot about attendance. I didn't really need an attendance record, so naturally I forgot to ask her if she'd done her task. I was a really strict taskmaster.

"Teacher, here." Camille handed me an index card a few days later.

"What's this?" I asked as I inspected the writing. It was a chart with all the names of the students in Guitar Club. She had marked an "X" for those in attendance that day. I was impressed. I had a very good assistant. Punctual, eager, and helpful. She offered to carry my music books and helped move instruments to the practice room.

"Assistant Camille! Stickers!" I'd call out, and she'd come over and give the designated student the sticker they'd just earned for playing their song. She followed me around class with a high sense of responsibility. Sticker giving was an enviable job.

Camille no longer lived on the sidelines, but she still watched the students with an interest that was more than innocent admiration. She actually paid attention to what was being done. I finally sat her down, momentarily revoked her assistant duties, and put a guitar in her lap.

"Here's how to play a chord," I began, and she accepted her new role as both guitar student and Assistant Camille.

~~~

I didn't realize just how attached I'd become to the Philippines until my final months of service when I played hostess to several visitors. I wasn't just attached, I was in love. It was as if the Philippines had become my lover, and I was introducing this new relationship to my family for the first time. Unfortunately, the Philippines was not being cooperative. A nine-hour bus ride to Baguio that was supposed to be six, uncooperative and abnormal weather for that time of year, and slower than usual traffic all gave the Philippines a bad impression to my family, which sent me reeling in anxiety.

*Come on, Philippines! Show them who you really are.*

"It's not usually like this," I told my mom and younger sister as I nudged the Philippines in the ribs.

"Everything seems good to us," my mom replied cheerily.

"Yeah, this is fun!" my sister agreed.

"Normally when the sun is out, this lookout is very beautiful," I explained as I peered into the foggy terrain. Drops of rain fell from the sky.

*Philippines, we need to talk.* I frowned in disapproval.

With every new visitor, I felt compelled to over-educate them about Filipino culture—the best foods to eat, the most beautiful places to visit, fun and exciting activities, and all the unique cultural mannerisms and Tagalog words. Most tourists could spot the most obvious things first, as I did when I first arrived in country. The broken-down houses, the dirty streets, and the dangerous driving. But I felt it was my duty to teach them *everything* about the Philippines and why I had fallen in love.

"You have to try the bananas! They are to die for."

"They're just bananas. We have bananas in America too."

"Yes, but they're *Philippine* bananas."

Or, "You have to try this mountain-roasted coffee."

"It tastes like regular coffee to me."

"But it's *Sagada* coffee. It came from the Cordillera mountains!"

Or, "Just wait until you watch the native dancing...You have to try this restaurant...The local market is just amazing...You're gonna love Pancit Canton instant noodles!"

After acting as tour guide on several visits from friends and family, I began to see myself in a new light. I was still a learner and a seeker, yes, but I had also begun to be the *teacher*. Just as my older guitar students had transitioned from student to teacher during our arts camp last summer, I too had transformed. I gathered confidence from this new role.

"How do you say hello in Filipino?" my older sister asked as we walked through the streets of Baguio. She and her husband were visiting for vacation.

I grinned. "Well, there are many ways. You could just say hello, or *kumusta*, which basically means 'how are you?'" I began.

"Oh yeah, I remember that. Kumusta."

"But then you could also greet people with questions like, 'Where are you going?' or 'Where did you come from?' or even 'Have you eaten yet?'"

"Have you eaten yet? Nice!" she laughed. "That's like what grandma used to say."

"What does *na* mean?" my brother-in-law asked as we passed a sign that read "Ice cream na!"

"It means now," I explained. "That sign means 'Have ice cream now!'"

"Oh, yeah?" He found that amusing. "So then, beer na!"

We all laughed.

For a long time during my service in the Philippines, I felt caught between two different worlds. The one where I used to live in America and the one where I was now living in the Philippines. My service began with the sense that I had spent the majority of my life missing out on a cultural upbringing that I could not define. It was as if all other Filipino Americans had somehow gotten a pre-boxed experience, and I was the only one lacking. But after my Philippine immersion, I found that I knew more about life there and its culture than many of my Filipino American friends. When I told them stories about the

Philippines, they'd be surprised, shocked, disgusted, or ready to laugh at the strange cultural differences I had encountered. I'd gone from one end of the spectrum to the other. *Wait, when did this happen?*

These epiphany moments were coming to me more often. Either I was finally learning these things, or it just took time before I was able to see it. One particular learning moment stuck in my memory. It was when Kenneth and I were sitting outside rehearsing a song in Tagalog for an upcoming performance. I was still self-conscious about my accent because the kids were continually making fun of me for it, so as I sang, I worried about how I sounded.

"My accent is bad, no?"

"What accent, Teacher?"

"Don't I have an American accent?"

"No, Teacher. You don't."

He was mistaken. I *did* have an American accent. But because he knew me, not as a stranger but as someone who was a meaningful part of his daily life, he didn't notice it anymore. It didn't matter to him. It was then that I finally felt a true sense of belonging. Not because I didn't have an accent, but because it didn't matter whether I had an accent or not. I was accepted for who I was: teacher, ate, neighbor, mentor, friend.

## 30

# IN BETWEEN TWO WORLDS

The lazy afternoon light lingered over me as I drifted in the hammock, swaying gently back and forth. The mountains stood in the distance as tranquil as always, their sloping curves and irregular roughness disappearing into the sky, layers upon layers, fading from dark blue into light gray, almost translucent, silhouetted against a fiery orange-flooded sea.

Several drops of rain fell on my toes. Then, in mere seconds, the whole valley was filled with a gray curtain of mist and livid rain. But the noise of thunderous, cascading drops didn't unnerve me even for a second. To hear the frenzied chaos of water splattering on the cement houses, the corrugated metal roofs, the gravel streets, the pine trees, and the banana leaves had become a source of comfort just as much as hearing the wild mountain wind blow fiercely through the valleys in the cool Baguio winters. As I watched the rain in contented stillness, the wind shifted, and I found myself covered with a confused flurry of spray. Time to head inside.

The whole sky darkened, and thunder announced its presence behind threatening, imminent clouds of mysterious gray swirling into black. The storm continued to sweep across the hills, slowly enveloping the mountains and swallowing their tall, forlorn peaks with a hungry menace. Only the houses closest to me could be seen; everything else was lost in a screen of gray water.

I loved thunderstorms during the hotter months in the Philippines. The sticky humidity of the day would turn into cool rain-soaked evenings filled with dancing, energetic streaks of purple lightning and cranky thunder echoing throughout the night. Those thunderstorms made their appearance almost every single evening, and my balcony was like a viewing screen to the world.

As I lounged in the hammock on my balcony, I'd sometimes think about my old life back in America—now a faded and fuzzy dream—in which I had wonderful conveniences like hot showers, flushing toilets, and electric clothes dryers. I was free to drive wherever I liked, whenever I pleased. I could eat American peanut butter and pizza with real cheese. I could go out for a jog in my neighborhood without being stared at. Retail stores were spacious wonders of immaculate organization.

But in the Philippines, I lived another way. Rain meant life and vigor. Cooking involved exotic dishes made from fresh ingredients at the open-air market. Communicating was exasperating, but smiles could tell you everything. I became everyone's big sister. Pandesal, laundry soap, and 3-in-1 coffee sachets were easily purchased at every street corner. I rode strange and sometimes dangerous modes of transportation that could whisk me off to enchanting places capable of fulfilling my lust for travel and adventure. My lifestyle was so different from what it used to be. It wasn't worse, it wasn't better, it was just different. I tried to imagine what I'd tell people when I got back. How would I ever tell my story? How could I explain the world I had encountered? I thought this over quite a bit in my remaining time, especially while visiting new areas of the country.

Just a few months before I was set to leave, I went with some volunteers on a caving expedition on the northeast side of Luzon.

"Let's go," said the kuya guide as he mounted his motorbike. We hopped on the kuyas' motorbikes and gripped their shoulders with fear and excitement. My stomach flipped as we set off. Paved roads turned to gravel, then to dirt. Rice fields stretched out on either side of us as we sped past. Delicate green shoots danced like ribbons in the breeze. Baby mountain peaks stood alert in the distance with their heads held high as the early morning sunshine warmed their rough shoulders. The steady rhythm of tire against dirt road provided a sense of comfort, and my tensed nerves soon gave way to exhilaration. I released an inward laugh of defiance, thrill, and joy all in one. As we raced through the backroads, that wild Philippine air gripped my senses and sunshine kindled my soul.

The dirt road narrowed to a muddy dike, so we dismounted to walk the rest of the way down a long, steep hill. At the bottom we were greeted by another kuya who supplied us with a large rice sack full of steamed corn for merienda snacks. I fueled up for the journey by devouring two cobs, and then we set off at last for our destination of the day—an underground river.

It was a precarious hike with no paths, no rails, no stepping stones, and no bridges. Just rough terrain and an invisible trail that was known only to our guide. We followed Kuya Cave Guide as best as we could, picking our way up the sides of the riverbank then crossing the river to the other side for better footing. Sometimes we swam our way up the stream, climbed up over a small buildup of rocks, and then swam upriver again. At last we reached a spot where we could no longer climb up by land or river. A giant waterfall loomed in our path. I wondered if this was the cave entrance.

"Let's climb up," Kuya Cave Guide said as he motioned toward the waterfall.

We all looked at him in disbelief. His partner demonstrated it to us first by jumping to the rocks near the bottom, and then he scaled his way to the top of the cliff by grasping hand and footholds through streaming water. We cheered for him, and he motioned for us to follow. One by one we skirted up past the rushing water, both kuyas assisting in pulling us up.

"Oh, you know," my friend joked at the top. "Climbing up waterfalls. Just another day in the Philippines." I smiled and looked down at the water below, eddying and cascading as it traveled down the river, flowing elegantly into pool after pool like a fancy fountain.

After making our way farther up the river, we arrived at the cave entrance, which was barely noticeable from the exterior. With nothing but the beams of a few headlamps, we progressed into the water-filled cave, hopping across flat rocks that were like mysterious floating islands in the darkness. The noise of the rushing river filled the cave with whispering echoes as it gushed unseen in the dark.

As we explored further, we reached a lookout rock jutting straight up out of the water. It was that to which we all clung, peering into a large cavern, an ocean of darkness and water melting into one. Kuya Cave Guide's swinging light beams illuminated various-sized stalactites as well as a waterfall pouring forth from an ominous dark opening.

Back outside the cave, some of the locals had prepared lunch for us near the riverside. The steaming pot held native chicken cooked with green papaya in ginger soup. It was a traditionally made *tinola*, a dish that had become as homey and comforting to me as chicken noodle soup in America. I ladled a generous serving over the bed of rice on my tin plate and began shoveling it into my mouth. I loved meals like these. All you needed were a few pots of tinola and rice and you could feed a large crowd. It embodied community, the coming together of people who all shared the same meal. Everyone was fed; everyone was happy.

After lunch, we journeyed back to the trailhead where the motorbike kuyas were waiting to take us home. They still needed us to walk the narrow muddy hill by foot, so they drove ahead while we followed on the dirt road.

"At least the ground has dried out now so the motorbikes won't have trouble in any mud like they did when we first came in," I told my friend ahead of me. I surveyed the hard caked ground with joy. Then, a few seconds after the words left my mouth, large drops of rain began to splatter on the ground.

"Noooooo!" I groaned. I had spoken too soon.

During the rainy season, when thick pellets of water begin falling like that, you knew a heavy downfall was imminent. The motorbike kuyas panicked and moved quickly to roar up the hill as fast as the narrow rough path would allow. Within minutes they were stuck as the rain fell hard in torrential Philippine style. Soon there was a thunderclap, a bolt of lightning, and then a steady flow of brown water rushed downward, threatening to trap us all. There was no option but to keep making our way up the hill to higher ground.

*I guess we still have one final waterfall to climb.* I had to laugh to myself as I plodded upward. Slippery flip-flops were no longer an option, so I mushed through the mud and grass in my bare feet, slipping and finding little traction. The rain continued to fall, and although I was completely soaked through, I still couldn't help but laugh at the hilarity of the situation. *Of course, this would happen to us. Bahala na!*

The downpour subsided after an hour or two, giving way to pockets of mist and fog drifting over the sloping, tree-covered mountains. I reached into my bag for my camera only to discover that it had been soaked as well. My phone had been luckier, but its camera had fogged up and took only blurry, white-streaked photos.

*What happened to the motorbike kuyas?* No one in our group had seen them for two hours. Last we saw of them, they were struggling to move their bikes through the mud far behind us. Most of us had made it to the crest of a hill after hiking up the now mud-filled "road." Eventually, as we reached the point of exhaustion, we came to a main intersection and a small motorbike with a sidecar passed by.

"Kuya! Can we ride with you?" we hollered as we waved him down.

The kuya nodded toward his sidecar, and a few of us climbed in. I sat in the sidecar, which had no bottom, just a few slats covered with a tarp, while my two friends sat on the sidecar rails. We all endured a bumpy, jolt-ridden drive to town. The others in our group caught a ride on another vehicle that passed, and all of us regrouped back in town. Completely soaked, we resembled mud-caked monsters.

"Where are the motorbike kuyas? Did they ever make it?"

"Maybe we should send someone back to find them," someone suggested. That was when the motorbike kuyas finally made their appearance, roaring down the road toward us as we cheered collectively.

After trips like these, it was hard to envision my life back in the States, where daily living did not involve muddy escapades, rice fields, and large pots of soup cooked over a campfire. Actually, more than the crazy travel adventures, it was even harder to imagine life in America without the normal everyday routine I had established and had become accustomed to—the little things that made the Philippines a place I could finally call my home. The triumph of shopping in the market without speaking English, the earnest kids I worked with at school, the way everyone in the neighborhood knew who I was.

"Hi, Ate Debs!"

"Good morning, Teacher!"

"Hi, Ate Devs."

Knock-knock.

"Teacher Debs, can you teach me something difficult?"

Sometimes my life in the Philippines felt like I was living in superlatives—small victories felt like BIG triumphs. Making a new friend felt like winning the lottery. Learning how to cook a local dish made me feel like I was the best chef in the world. Along with the small victories, I learned to appreciate, celebrate, and love the culture, people, and way of life as well.

I'd grown to love the Philippines, and now I found my thoughts continually churning and casting doubt on the day I'd return back to the US. *One day, will this life I made here become a distant memory?* I had been so fixated on learning how to live in the Philippines with confidence and familiarity that I'd forgotten about the time when my world would flip and I'd find myself once again living on American soil.

I had a dream one night that I went back home after my service and, although I was surrounded by people, I felt lonely. Like I didn't fit in. No one understood what I had been through or the changes I felt. Everyone went on with their lives, and I was left feeling lost and out of place. *Was there a way to make my two worlds unite?*

## 31

## HALO-HALO

"You know you're Filipino when it gets super hot out and the first thing that pops into your mind is how much you're craving halo-halo," I texted to Ben. "Seriously, what has my life become?"

He responded with, "Yeah, I've been getting my fix at Chow King lately."

Halo-halo, the unique slushy dessert medley of fruit, jellies, beans, corn, purple *ube* ice-cream, and shaved ice sounds strange to foreigners—most tend to be dissuaded by the thought of all those bizarre tastes mixed together—but it grows on you. It's the most popular snack to eat during summer months when the entire Philippines feels like an oven ready to broil a chicken on high.

"Halo-halo!" children call out from behind makeshift street stands. They grab little plastic cups premade with candy-like jellies and purple ube jam and then top it off with fresh shaved ice. Some vendors grate a block of ice right in front of you using a metal hand shaver. Summer is when ice at my neighborhood sari-sari store is in scarce supply.

"Let's go get some," I texted back to Ben. "My house is so hot right now!"

"I'm down for halo-halo! See you there."

My little cement block house could get a nice cross breeze if I kept both doors open. But even then, the heat would make you drowsy. Just a little nap, you'd reason to yourself. No harm in taking five minutes for a snooze. And then you'd be out for the rest of the afternoon. When you finally came out of your heat-induced sleep, your first thought would be, "Where can I get some halo-halo?" Yup. Purple slushy desserts and Philippine summers went together like glazed bananas on a stick. These were the best things in life.

Just a few weeks before, the internet kuya had come by to fix some wiring, and I sat near the open door watching as the workers in my house adjusted various cables. There was no breeze. Something wasn't connecting right, and the kuyas started conversing in one corner of the room. Then they went outside, leaving just the manager behind. I sat waiting while he worked away. Still no breeze. The kuya read through a stack of papers then reached into his work bag and pulled out another stack of documents. He read through those too. After five minutes of watching this, I asked him, "Kuya, where did they go? Are they fixing something outside?"

"Oh, no. Dey just went to get halo-halo," he replied nonchalantly, then went back to his work. Well, I guess it *was* sweltering outside. Makes sense. Halo-halo break it is.

Things I've learned thus far in the Philippines:

1. A guitar will help you do useful things.
2. Halo-halo is an acceptable excuse for a break.
3. Staring at people *is* OK.
4. What is a meal without rice?
5. Patience is a virtue. I have *some*.
6. Google will help you be an expert in anything.
7. I'll get there when I get there.

8. Bahala na.

~~~

My three years in the Philippines were drawing to a close. Three years of curvy mountain roads, slushy purple desserts, and videoke at nine in the morning. Three years of pointing with my lips and asking random strangers on the street where they were going. At last, I'd made it through this roller coaster journey. At last, my time of waiting to discover my true identity would come to fruition. I could smell the sweet fragrance of ripened understanding. It was all just waiting there, ready to be plucked from the magical self-identity tree of knowledge. Patience was a virtue. I had *some*.

"Hello!" I heard a voice call through my open door. Mariella's mom peeked through the crack. "Ma'am Debs, have you eaten yet?"

"Not yet."

"Come eat now! It's Mariella's birthday. Come downstairs. Dere's a party." She led the way down the cement steps into their little apartment.

"Mestiza!" Mariella called out when I entered.

"Hi, Mari! Happy birthday!"

"Here, you eat now," Mariella's auntie said as she handed me a plate.

I sat on a plastic mint-colored chair eating pancit noodles while Mariella's dad asked me questions. "So, you are half Pilipino?"

"Yes, my dad is Filipino."

"So, how long you live here, eh?"

"Here you have cake now." Mariella's lola pushed a slice of purple ube cake onto my plate.

"I've been here almost three years."

"When you go back to America?"

"Soon, in a few weeks."

"Oh, bery nice, mestiza."

*Mestiza? Come on! Even now, after all this time, they still call me mestiza? Half Filipino, half foreigner.*

"Mestiza also means beautiful, Ate Debs," Carmelita informed me one day when she heard me talking about little Mariella. "There are many Filipinos who consider someone who is half Filipino and half foreign to be much more beautiful than a full Filipino."

*Oh? Beautiful? Well, then. Call me mestiza anytime.*

Still, I was not satisfied. I came to realize one warm Sunday morning as I drifted in my hammock that my dreams of unearthing an epiphany moment, finding that perfectly boxed identity, had been dashed to the ground. Two identities into one? No matter how I worked it out in my head, it didn't add up the way I wanted it to. Half Filipino, half foreigner. Half Filipino, half American. Full Filipino, full American. Two wholes did not equal one whole. Fighting to cram both cultural identities into one box became just as difficult as keeping the ants from attacking my pandesal bread left out on the counter.

There were times when I knew I was being hypocritical, my identities contradicting and fighting against themselves. I wasn't Filipino *enough*, or I was *too* Filipino. Sometimes I wanted to be recognized as an American, while other times I hoped to fit in and be seen as a Filipino. Lingering too long on either end of the spectrum would leave me feeling like I was ignoring the other parts of me that I knew I identified with. I lived regularly in the tension between these thoughts. Finding a balance was the only way I would be able reconcile all aspects of myself and my cultural identities.

Looking back, I recalled a conversation I had during one of my first few weeks in the neighborhood. I wasn't in the mood for playing guitar or practicing Tagalog with Ate Malaya, so I sat outside my house and just watched the tambay men engaged in a chess game. A thunderstorm had just subsided, and in the cool, crisp night I zipped my sweatshirt all the way up. My friend David sat nearby, watching the movements of the game. Then he inhaled his cigarette thoughtfully, trails of curling gray smoke disappearing into the night air, and turned to address me. "So, you're Pilipino?"

"Yes, but I'm Filam."

"Oh, so you're half Pilipino, half American."

"No, actually I'm full American. But I'm also Filipino."

"So, your mother must be Pilipino?"

"No, my dad is the Filipino one. He's from Iloilo City."

"Oh, then your mother is American?"

"Yes, she is part Slovenian, Irish, and French."

David looked both puzzled and amused at that last answer, perhaps trying to calculate or analyze that new piece of information inside his head. "Oh…so what does that make you?"

"Halo-halo," I joked, thinking about the coconut jellies, corn, and ice cream swirling together inside a goblet of purple liquid. A little of this, a little of that. Mix-mix. Although it had originally been meant as a silly joke to describe my mix of identities, over the years it had grown on me. Halo-halo wasn't a defining answer, but it was a good way to explain the ambiguity of my identity. I am definitely mix-mix, but it was figuring out the ingredients in my own halo-halo that I found to be the most difficult. Add a little bit of Filipino, a lot of American. Stir it around and add condensed milk. It was not as easy as it looked.

I had come to the Philippines with the mindset that I would simply learn more about the culture of my dad and his family. It began as a journey to discover my roots, learn about my heritage, and understand a culture I had always wished to be a part of. Naively, I was simply looking for a name, a label to identify with. Instead, I encountered the culture much more intimately than I ever expected, facing each new challenge in a very personal way. Through integration, I found a part of myself I didn't know existed. The longer I lived in the Philippines, the more I was able to discover new things about myself and reconcile my identity as both Filipino and American. In reality, it wasn't that I had missed out on something but that I had yet to discover it within myself. I had become a part of the Philippines, and now it had become a part of me.

I realized in the end that there was no perfect box. I was American, yet I had roots in the Philippines and had now learned a lot about Filipino culture. I could see more clearly what it meant to be Filipino compared to what it meant to be American, and discovered that I didn't quite fit into either category all that well. There was an ambiguous place somewhere in the middle. That is where I found myself. I was neither one nor the other, but both, intertwined so tightly that those knots would never be untangled. I was able to identify with and could embody both cultures while remaining completely true to myself.

Throughout my three years in the Philippines, I experienced the sensation of walking back and forth along a bridge between two beloved cultures. Now I found myself standing somewhere in the middle of that bridge. I came to understand that finding the source of my self-identity would always mean creating a bridge between two different worlds. Walking back and forth across that bridge in perpetual movement would become my ultimate journey. I am proud to call myself a Filipino American and feel privileged to represent a combination of different cultures. It's OK to have many names and identities. I finally acknowledged that there isn't one thing that strictly defines me; I am a multifaceted, complex person and now prefer to be seen that way. Ever since I began a search for my roots, my desire to understand more about who I am has only increased. I'm excited to see where that search for self-identity will lead me next.

## 32

# WHERE ARE YOU GOING, ATE?

I lay on my bed unmotivated, contemplating the organization and packing tasks sitting before me. My time to return to America had finally come, and I was procrastinating. Maybe I was in denial. Everything I had accumulated or bought in the last three years, everything that had made up my life lay in odd mounds scattered throughout my house. I had three pile options: give away, keep, and trash. I hoisted myself up and picked out items at random, executing final decisions. *OK, time to get this done.*

Two pairs of jeans, still intact. *Keep.* Three pairs impaled with holes, rips, and shredded edges. *Trash.* Tin box of earrings. *Keep.* Hair dryer. *Keep.* Dinner plates and bowls. *Give away.* Melted candle wax leftover from the last power outage. *Trash.* Moldy pillowcase. *Trash.* It became easier now. Moldy folder of old language practice sheets. *Trash.* Dictionary of English and Tagalog. *Keep.*

I went through my closet to find a few pieces of clothing that could still be considered respectable in public. *Keep.* All the others I tossed on my bed. They were stained, worn, and stretched from constant overuse, sweat, travel, handwashing, and wringing. I considered for a moment if I shouldn't also create a burn pile. Envisioning those filthy things incinerated brought glee to my face. *Nah. Trash. Not even decent enough to give away.* Boots I bought for insanely cheap at the street market. *Give away.* Two pairs of Converse, black and gray. *Give away.* Can of Raid. *No need for that anymore, thank God! Give away.*

Handwoven tapis skirt. *Definitely keep.* I adored the brightly colored woven fabrics. That skirt had become a reminder of my home here. I remember buying my tapis when our school celebrated *Buwan ng Wika*, the annual Philippines' cultural celebration. Each year, the students performed traditional songs and dance numbers to celebrate their heritage. I had prepared my choir class to sing the traditional Ilocano song "Manang Biday," which was well known in the mountains and Ilocos regions. I surprised my students by coming to the performance wearing a tapis.

"Wow! *Igorot siya!* She's a mountain girl!" I overheard one of the parents exclaim as I walked by.

*I am? I am! I'm a mountain girl now.* I tucked the tapis carefully inside my suitcase.

One French Press. *Keep.* I used it almost every single day to brew my morning coffee—Sagada roast, Kalinga, Benguet Blend—and then sit quietly soaking in the morning rays of sunlight. Oftentimes, drinking coffee brought back specific memories. I recalled cups I'd once enjoyed that were forever wrapped up in the events of that moment. My best coffee memories were the simple ones like afternoon chats with my host mom in Baguio, late night coffee with friends at our local hangout spot, or merienda time at my office. I'd never forget that one day in Banaue when I was waiting for my bus back to Baguio, and all I did was drink coffee, read, and stare dreamily out the window at the picturesque rice terraces sloping down the mountainsides. *Definitely keep.*

Map of the Philippines. I paused for a moment. Scanning the terrain, I brushed my finger lightly against each place I had visited: Manila, Sagada, Banaue, Batad, Pagudpud, Iloilo, Batangas, Dumaguete, Siquijor, Bohol, Palawan, Cagayan, Zambales, Mount Pulag, Vigan, Marinduque. The list went on. I had covered quite a bit of the country. *Keep.* Then I noticed that the paper was faded and corroded with white mold. *Looks like it's the trash pile after all.*

I reached up and took down a sticker from the wall that I had brought with me when I first arrived three years ago. The sticker, in the shape of the state of Oregon with a big heart in the center, was meant to remind me of home. *Where was home for me now?* I wasn't sure that I had an exact answer for that anymore.

The packing and giving-away catharsis method continued throughout the rest of the week as I began to say my goodbyes and slowly detach myself from my life in the community. Team English showed up at my door, his eyes darting around to the vastly changed environment inside my living room. Suitcases, bags, and junk piles were dumped everywhere. Boxes and mounds of household items were heaped in one corner, ready to give away.

"I've been packing," I explained. "Jonas, I have something I want to give you." I went into my room and brought out my guitar. I handed it to him, ignoring the surprise and shock etched into his face. "I'm confident that you'll use it, and it will help you continue to practice, and you're really very good," I stammered.

"Thank you, Teacher. Thank you so much!" he exclaimed. We both just stood there not knowing what to say. I eventually remembered to take a snapshot of him with the guitar. In the photo, he stands very calm, still the face of a child, but I can see how he has grown since the time I first met him.

"I'll take good care of it," he promised and then turned to leave.

~~~

On my last day of work, I went down to the schoolrooms to visit my students. "I came to say goodbye. Today is my last day," I told them as they packed up their bags. I gave high fives and hugs, and there were plenty of smiles and I-will-miss-yous to go around. Then I stood there awkwardly. Awkward always found its way into saying goodbye for me, but I wasn't the only one. In the corridor after class, I happened to notice Kenneth standing beside me. He wasn't looking at me, just hanging around, head bent down.

"Kenneth, it's my last day today. I came to say goodbye."

He looked up at me briefly and nodded. *Was his face red?* I held out my hand for a high five, but then all of a sudden he came at me, head still bowed, and gave me a hug around the waist with his tiny arms. He looked up once more, and I was sure of it that time. His face was all puffy and red. Eyes watery. My heart melted.

"Aww. I'm gonna miss you," I told him before he ran off, head still lowered.

For after school, the staff had prepared a little *despedida*, a goodbye party. Jonas showed up, and when I saw him enter the room, I called out, "Team English! What's up!" and gave him a high five. He returned it bashfully then handed me a letter.

*To my beautiful Teacher Deborah,*

> *I wanted to say THANK YOU SOOO MUCH for everything you teach us, for your long patience in teaching us. Sorry for the times that we are naughty in our practice. Thank you for being a big part in my music life, if it's not because of you, maybe until now I don't*

*have that much knowledge in playing guitar. Thank you teacher for the guitar, I will take care of it. Now that you're coming back to America we'll surely miss you. Hope that one day you'll visit us again. We wish you all the best in life. TAKE CARE ALWAYS AND GOD BLESS YOU. WE LOVE YOU!!!*

*Your only one handsome guitarist, Jonas*

I smiled at Jonas then gave him another high five. "Aww…thanks Jonas." Then I tucked his letter carefully inside my bag. Several other students and their parents had given me similar notes, cards, and texts throughout the week and I felt so touched by their words. One of my favorite messages was a goodbye poem composed by Samuel which he texted to me one evening:

*Teacher debs thank u.*
*We learned many thing from u.*
*We are so thankful,*
*and very joyful*
*that u came into our life,*
*and make it livelier.*

Although I hated goodbyes, I loved their messages—I saved them inside an envelope to take home with me as if they were the last scraps of memories I would have of them.

As a part of the despedida party, there were embarrassing speeches and songs dedicated to Teacher Debs. The program also included several musical acts—Jonas and I performed one of our usual songs. We nodded to each other like longtime bandmates as we began to strum our last performance together. At the end of the night, he gave me one last goodbye before he walked off into the evening, white-and-black-striped collared polo, carefree stride, shoulders swaying, head bouncing.

"Here. Dis is from all of us, your friends," Ma'am Ligaya said as she handed me a package. I smiled at her, remembering our cooking lesson a few weeks back. Ma'am Ligaya and Ma'am Anna had taught me how to make *puto* and *biko*, both sweet rice desserts. I was so proud of my work in the kitchen that I kept telling everyone at work the next day how I had become a puto and biko "master." The two moms laughed in delight. We also joked about how Ma'am Ligaya accidentally burned the bottom of the rice for the biko. Ma'am Ligaya held the camera while Ma'am Anna took the crispy burned section and pretended to eat it like a giant cookie. Again, they burst into laughter with big infectious smiles. But with Ma'am Ligaya, it was always laughter.

"Thank you!" I smiled at Ma'am Ligaya as I clutched the package. Then I tore at the paper to reveal a beautiful handwoven turquoise-colored purse. "Thank you so much for everything!"

~~~

At home, I gathered and sorted the remainder of my things, shoving piles to various corners of my house. I picked up the large tin pot that I used to heat my water in the mornings for my bucket bath. *Give away.* A nonstick wok used to cook a majority of my one-pot meals, the handle gone slightly awry. *Give away.* A one-burner gas stove. *Give away.*

Knock-knock. I knew exactly who it was going to be.

Knock-knock.

As I opened my rusted door, I saw Jayden standing there, bashful as ever. I pushed my suitcases aside and cleared a space for him to sit at my kitchen table so we could hang out. We sat and talked, played some word games, and listened to a few songs on my laptop. Sometimes we just stared outside at the mountains. It was just like what we usually did, except this time it felt different. There was that lingering sense of finality. But instead of facing it with dread, I found that simply sitting together in those last days was sufficient enough for me. Simple was better. That was how it had always been with Jayden and me—it seemed a fitting way for the two of us to say goodbye.

"OK...well...goodbye, Ate Debs," he murmured.

"Goodbye, Jayden! I'll miss you!"

"Miss you too. OK...bye." He waved and then walked down the road to his house, tugging at his gray T-shirt, turning around every few steps to wave again.

~~~

I sat alone with the remnants of the life I had lived in the Philippines, neatly packed and ready to go. Three years of my life tucked into three pieces of luggage. It was time to go home.

Most people assume that at the end of your service as a Peace Corps volunteer you'll give yourself a pat on the back for having served the country and changed the lives of the people who live there, and then you'll move on to other more important areas of your life. But the opposite had become my reality—the experience changed *me*. There was no going back to an ordinary life, and even if I could, I wouldn't have wanted to. Life back in America was going to look a lot different for me.

I finally moved out of my cement block house stuck on the side of a mountain. The taxi-driver kuya helped me hoist my suitcases up into the trunk of the vehicle.

"San Lorenzo Barangay," I told him. I'd be staying with my host family for a few days before I traveled to Manila, and from there I'd fly back to America. We drove up the giant hill that had given me strong glute muscles walking to work every day. We passed the winding curves of the mountain highway. Two curves, then the little market. Round a bigger curve, past the dumpsite. Then open fields and a large valley to the right. Slow columns of smoke drifted up from the valley. I could hear a distant call of the balut kuya as he wandered the neighborhood selling his duck eggs.

"Baluuuuuuuut! Baluuuuuuuut!"

~~~

Francyn and I lounged on the living room floor and talked about America. "Maybe one day I will come visit you, Ate Debs," she said. It was my last evening at my host family's house in Baguio.

"Yes, come visit me!"

I looked over and saw Khurt hovering near the doorframe, hesitant to enter the room. "Khurt, come here. I need to tell you something."

"Why can't you just tell me here?" he asked.

"It's a secret."

He slipped behind the jackets hanging next to the doorway and just stood there.

"Khurt, come here!"

"You can't see me now. I'm invisible."

"No, you're not. I can still see your legs."

"My god! I forgot about my legs!" He came out, resigned to having been caught being invisible. He sat down next to me. "So, what's your secret?"

I hugged him hard and whispered, "I'm gonna miss you! Are you gonna miss me?"

"Yes!" he exclaimed. I hugged him harder.

"But why are you leaving? Where are you going?"

"I'm going back to America."

"But you'll come back again next month, right?"

"No…"

"Well, then just come back in two months."

"Hmmm, we'll see…"

Early in the morning I slipped out of Baguio City, quiet and reflective as I leaned against the bus window. I gazed at the mountains upon mountains and the twinkling city lights on the hills. Just like that, my life in the Philippines—one that oftentimes felt like a dream—was gone, left behind in the drifting fog and illumination of the city glow.

"Goodbye, Baguio," I whispered as the bus zigzagged down the mountain road with me as the passenger for the last time.

~~~

Since returning to the United States, I've developed friendships with many other Filipinos just like me from various mixed backgrounds—Filipino Mexican American, Filipino Canadian, Filipino Hawaiian American—who share the same experience of feeling caught in the middle of two or more cultures. It's a tension they've lived with throughout their lives, moving back and forth between diverse family backgrounds and heritages. But many have found that by accepting a fluid and shifting identity they can also benefit from the cultural richness of multiple backgrounds. While confusing at times, it can also be a gift. I finally realized that my tension between two cultural identities was completely normal. Although each new person I met had their own unique experiences, we were still connected by the common denominator of our somewhere-in-the-middle narratives.

It's empowering to know that there are others out there just like me who have journeyed in search of their own identities and have also found themselves wandering the bridge between two or more worlds. Even now, years after living the Philippines, I still walk that bridge, wavering between a longing to keep Filipino culture alive in my life and a yearning to just stop worrying about it. *Bahala na.* I let my Filipino roots and my American life intermingle as much or as little as they want. I am content with being in the middle, and I have also accepted the various names that people use to describe me. Whether mestiza, half Filipino, mix-mix, halo-halo, Filam, or Filipino American, I am not defined by *just* a name. I am the only one who can define me, and I will continue doing so for the rest of my life, floating in and out of my cultural identities in the same way the clouds floated through the valley below my mountains upon mountains.

## THE END

# Acknowledgements

While I still lived in the Philippines, I used to go to a coffee shop every Sunday afternoon, sipping away as I wrote out the stories of my life there. That process made me realize just how much I had fallen in love with the Philippines and how grateful I was for my experience as a volunteer. It transformed my life in ways I can't even begin to describe and changed my perspective on the way I see the world.

I am so thankful to all the people who appear in this book—students, friends, co-workers, host families, volunteers, strangers—who welcomed me into their lives and slowly became a normal part of my life in the Philippines. There were many others that I was not able to mention, and there were many stories I was not able to include (that would have made for one long book!) but I am so thankful for all the friendships I made during my time as a volunteer.

Thank you to my editor Christine Schmidt who enthusiastically dove into this project, going the extra mile to make my manuscript shine. Her encouraging words helped me persevere through the final editing stage and transform my passion project into a final book. I also want to give a shout out to Ivy Pangilinan for the amazing and colorful cover art design.

Many thanks to my family and friends who supported me along the way, providing much needed moral support, especially to those who read earlier drafts of the book including Rita, Ferch, Vanessa, Pamela, Alex, Chris, Angela, and my parents, to name a few. A special thanks to my mom—my cheerleader throughout—who read countless drafts and assisted with the editing process. And finally, to my husband who always gives me the encouragement and confidence to passionately pursue my dreams. Thank you!

## About the Author

Deborah Francisco Douglas is a writer, blogger, dreamer, and adventurer. She served three years in the Philippines as a Peace Corps volunteer (2011-2014) working on community development and youth outreach programs. As a Filipino American, Deborah's volunteer experience abroad connected her to a culture she had long desired to understand. When she returned to the United States, Deborah created the blog *Halo-Halo, Mix-Mix – Discovering the Filipino American Identity*, as a way to share her love of Filipino culture.

Deborah lives in sunny San Diego and loves hiking, reading, walks on the bay, and lazy mornings drinking coffee. *Somewhere in the Middle* is her debut memoir.

Visit her blog at www.halohalomixmix.com to learn more about Filipino culture, travel, and lifestyle.

Made in the USA
San Bernardino, CA
23 April 2019